Knitting

Easy Fun for Everyone

Mirror Image, page 109

HINKLER BOOKS

Knitting

Cover design: Hinkler Books Studio
Typesetting: Macmillan Publishing Solutions
Prepress: Graphic Print Group

Published in 2009 by Hinkler Books Pty Ltd
45–55 Fairchild Street
Heatherton VIC 3202 Australia
www.hinklerbooks.com

ISBN: 978 1 7418 3049 1
Printed and bound in China

Originally published by
Company's Coming Publishing Limited
2311-96 Street
Edmonton, Alberta, Canada T6N 1G3
Tel: 780-450-6223   Fax: 780-450-1857
www.companyscoming.com

THE COMPANY'S COMING STORY

Jean Paré grew up with an understanding that family, friends and home cooking are the key ingredients for a good life. A mother of four, Jean worked as a professional caterer for eighteen years, operating out of her home kitchen. During that time, she came to appreciate quick and easy recipes that call for everyday ingredients. In answer to mounting requests for her recipes, Company's Coming cookbooks were born, and Jean moved on to a new chapter in her career.

In the beginning, Jean worked from a spare bedroom in her home, located in the small prairie town of Vermilion, Alberta, Canada. The first Company's Coming cookbook, *150 Delicious Squares,* was an immediate bestseller. Today, with well over 100 titles in print, Company's Coming has earned the distinction of being the publisher of Canada's most popular cookbooks. The company continues to gain new supporters by adhering to Jean's 'Golden Rule of Cooking'—never share a recipe you wouldn't use yourself. It's an approach that works—millions of times over!

Company's Coming cookbooks are distributed throughout Canada, the United States, Australia and other international English-language markets. French-and Spanish-language editions have also been published. Sales to date have surpassed 25 million copies with no end in sight. Familiar and trusted in home kitchens around the world, Company's Coming cookbooks are highly regarded both as kitchen workbooks and as family heirlooms.

Company's Coming founder Jean Paré

Just as Company's Coming continues to promote the tradition of home cooking, now the same is true with crafting. Like cooking, successful crafts depend upon easy-to-follow instructions, readily available materials and enticing photographs of the finished products. Also like cooking, crafts are meant to be enjoyed in the home or cottage. Company's Coming Crafts, then, seems to be a natural extension from the kitchen into the family room or den.

Because Company's Coming operates a test kitchen and not a craft shop, we've partnered with a major North American craft publisher to assemble a variety of craft compilations exclusively for us. Our editors have been involved every step of the way. You can see the results for yourself in the book you're holding.

Company's Coming Crafts are for everyone—whether you're a beginner or a seasoned pro. What better gift could you offer than something you've made yourself? In these hectic days, people still enjoy crafting parties—whether it be knitting, card making, quilting or any of a wide range of crafts. Crafting brings family and friends together in the same way that a good meal tightens the bond between family and friends. Company's Coming is proud to support crafters with this new craft book series.

We hope you enjoy these easy-to-follow, informative, colourful books and that they will inspire your creativity! So don't delay—get crafty!

TABLE OF CONTENTS

A Word about Yarn 6 • Foreword 7 • General Instructions 8

Starburst Table Mat,
page 146

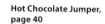

Hot Chocolate Jumper,
page 40

Rainbow Squares,
page 106

Make-In-a-Hurry Tabard,
page 52

Smiley Face Cardigan,
page 14

TABLE OF CONTENTS

Like Father, Like Son,
page 21

Monster Mania Pillows,
page 125

Weave a Little Colour,
page 62

Roll the Dice Tote Bag,
page 68

Strut Your Stuff,
page 12

A WORD ABOUT YARN

Each project in this book has been created with the yarns listed in the materials. The yarns have been graded according to their weight or category. This symbol ![1 SUPER FINE] will tell you what grade yarn to use.

Yarn Weight Symbol & Category Names	1 SUPER FINE	2 FINE	3 LIGHT	4 MEDIUM	5 BULKY	6 SUPER BULKY
Type of Yarns in Category	Sock, Fingering, Baby	Sport, Baby	DK, Light Worsted	Worsted, Afghan, Aran	Chunky, Craft, Rug	Bulky, Roving
Knit Gauge* Ranges in Stockinette Stitch to 10cm (4 inches)	21–32 sts	23–26 sts	21–24 sts	16–20 sts	12–15 sts	6–11 sts
Recommended Needle in Metric Size Range	2.25–3.25mm	3.25–3.75mm	3.75–4.5mm	4.5–5.5mm	5.5–8mm	8mm
Recommended Needle Canada/US Size Range	1 to 3	3 to 5	5 to 7	7 to 9	9 to 11	11 and larger

* GUIDELINES ONLY: The above reflect the most commonly used gauges and needle sizes for specific yarn categories.

If the yarn listed for the project is unavailable, choose a substitute of the same weight. **Always** knit a sample square to check that the gauge matches that of the project. Ask your local knitting club or wool store for assistance selecting the correct wool if you need advice. Many yarns are now available internationally through online knitting stores.

FOREWORD

The tremendous popularity of knitting today continues to astound us. Yarn companies have gone wild with yarns in gorgeous colours and textures. There are almost more kinds of yarn than you can count. To make use of these yarns, we've collected more than 70 easy-to-stitch designs, all waiting for you between the covers of our book.

Stylish sweaters, lightweight wraps and fabulous bags for women abound in this collection. A classic matching sweater set for father and son, or even mother and daughter, will easily become a favourite to knit for your family and friends.

Fun sweaters, cosy blankets and princess and prince royalty bibs for baby make perfect gifts for the precious young ones in your family or circle of friends. For those whose family includes cats or dogs, there are handsome dog jackets and a special pillow for your cat.

Favourites of knitters everywhere are cosy throws, wrap-me-up-in afghans, delightful baby blankets and soft pillows. Five or six of these are beginner level projects, and the rest are easy level except for the Maple Leaf throw that is intermediate level. Experienced knitters will find these projects so easy to knit that they'll want to knit several to have on hand for baby or housewarming gifts. The throws also make super knee warmers for the elderly.

A cheerful tea cosy will add a touch of whimsy to your table. Hot mats, place mats and textured face cloths are home accents you can make quickly to give as gifts. Place them in a basket with a selection of tea bags or special soaps. These quick-and-easy gifts will be much appreciated as shower gifts for the bride.

So, take out your knitting needles and yarn, select a design and enjoy hours of knitting pleasure. You'll have a relaxing time knitting, and your completed project will be enjoyed for years to come.

Checks & Stripes Twin Set, page 26

Fringe

Cut a piece of cardboard half as long as specified in instructions for strands plus 1.3cm (½ inch) for trimming. Wind yarn loosely and evenly around cardboard. When cardboard is filled, cut yarn across one end. Do this several times then begin fringing. Wind additional strands as necessary.

Single Knot Fringe

Hold specified number of strands for one knot together, fold in half. Hold project to be fringed with right side facing you. Use crochet hook to draw folded end through space or stitch indicated from right to wrong side.

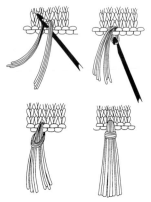

Pull loose ends through folded section.

Draw knot up firmly. Space knots as indicated in pattern instructions.

Double Knot Fringe

Begin by working Single Knot Fringe completely across one end of piece. With right side facing you and

working from left to right, take half the strands of one knot and half the strands of the knot next to it and knot them together.

Triple Knot Fringe

Work Double Knot Fringe across. With right side facing you, work from left to right tying a third row of knots.

Blanket Stitch

This stitch is worked along edge of piece. Bring needle up and make a counterclockwise loop. Take stitch as indicated, keeping the thread beneath the point of needle. Pull through to form stitch. Continue in same manner around outer edge.

Provisional Cast-On

The provisional cast-on has a variety of uses. It starts with a crochet chain on a crochet hook about the same size as the knitting needle. The chart given below shows crochet hooks that correspond most closely to knitting needle sizes.

Crochet Hook	Knitting Needle
3.5mm (E)	3.5mm (4)
3.75mm (F)	3.75mm (5)
4.25mm (G)	4mm (6)
5mm (H)	3mm (8)
5.5mm (I)	5.5mm (9)
6mm (J)	6mm (10)
6.5mm (K)	6.5mm (10½)

To work this type of cast-on, start with a crochet chain with one or two stitches more than the number of stitches to be cast on for the pattern you are working. If the edge is to be decorative or removed to work in the opposite direction, then the chain should be made with a contrasting colour.

Once the chain is completed, with a knitting needle, pick up and knit in the back bump of each chain (Photo 1) until the required number of stitches is on the needle. Continue to work the pattern as given in the instructions.

Some instructions indicate that the provisional cast-on be removed so the piece can be worked in the opposite direction. In this case, hold the work with the cast-on edge at the top. Undo one loop of the crochet chain, inserting the knitting needle into the stitch below the chain. (This stitch is on the original first row of knitting.) Continue to undo the crochet chain until all the stitches are on the needle (Photo 2). This provides a row of stitches ready to work in the opposite direction.

Twisted Cord

Items sometimes require a cord as a drawstring closing or strap. The number of lengths and weight of yarn determine the thickness of the cord.

To form the cord, hold the number of cords indicated together with matching ends. Attach one end to a doorknob or hook. Twist the other end in one direction until the length is tightly twisted and begins to kink.

Sometimes the lengths are folded in half before twisting. In this case the loose ends are attached to the doorknob and a pencil is slipped into the folded loop at the other end. Turn the pencil to twist the cord.

Once the cord is tightly twisted, continue to hold the twisted end while folding the yarn in the middle. Remove the end from the knob or hook and match the two ends, then release them allowing the cord to twist on itself.

Trim the cord ends to the desired length and knot each end. If the cord is woven through eyelets, it may be necessary to tie a second knot in the end to prevent it from slipping back through the eyelet opening.

3-Needle Bind Off

Use this technique for seaming two edges together, such as when joining a shoulder seam. Hold the edge stitches on two separate needles with right sides together.

With a third needle, knit together a stitch from the front needle with one from the back.

Repeat, knitting a stitch from the front needle with one from the back needle once more.

Slip the first stitch over the second.

Repeat, knitting a front and back pair of stitches together, then bind one off.

Crochet Class

For the times when you need a little crochet to trim or edge your knit project, look here.

Some knit items are finished with a crochet trim or edging. Below are some abbreviations used in crochet and a review of some basic crochet stitches.

Crochet Abbreviations

ch......................................chain stitch
dc...............................double crochet
hdc...................half double crochet
lp(s)..loop(s)
sc ....single crochet
sl st......................................slip stitch
yo...yarn over

Single Crochet (sc)

Insert the hook in the second chain through the centre of the V. Bring yarn over the hook from back to front.

Draw the yarn through the chain stitch and onto the hook.

Again bring yarn over the

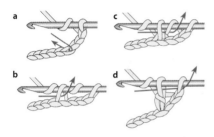

hook from back to front and draw it through both loops on hook.

For additional rows of single crochet, insert the hook under both loops of the previous stitch instead of through the centre of the V as when working into the chain stitch.

Double Crochet (dc)

Yo, insert hook in st, yo, pull through st, (yo, pull through 2 lps) 2 times.

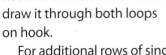

Reverse Single Crochet (reverse sc)

Working from left to right, insert hook under both loops of the next stitch to the right.

Bring yarn over hook from back to front and draw through both loops on hook.

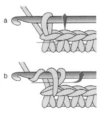

Slip Stitch (sl st)

Insert hook under both loops of the stitch, bring yarn over the hook from back to front and draw it through the stitch and the loop on the hook.

Cruising The Neighbourhood

Spot will step out in style in his business-like coat. Going to the park? It's also perfect for a doggie playdate.

DESIGN BY BONNIE FRANZ

EASY

Sizes
Dog's small (medium, large) instructions are given for smallest size, with larger sizes in parentheses. When only 1 number is given, it applies to all sizes.

Finished Measurements
Back width: 35.5 (43, 51)cm or 14 (17, 20) inches
Length: 38 (50, 62)cm or 15 (19¾, 24¾) inches

Materials
- Plymouth Encore Chunky 75 per cent acrylic/25 per cent wool bulky weight yarn (131 metres (143 yds)/100g per ball): 1 (2, 2) ball(s) navy heather #658 (MC), 1 ball grey #678 (CC)
- 5mm (size 8) circular needles at least 61cm (24 inches) long
- 6mm (size 10) circular needle at least 61cm (24 inches) long, or size needed to obtain gauge
- Tapestry needle
- 3 (2-cm/⅞-inch) buttons

Gauge
13 sts and 18 rows = 10cm/ 4 inches in St st with larger needles
To save time, take time to check gauge.

Stripe Pattern
Work following sequence in St st:
    5 rows MC, 1 row CC
    Rep these 6 rows for pat.

Pattern Notes
This coat is worked from side to side.

The circular needle allows you to work the Stripe Pattern from either side of fabric depending on where the necessary yarn is.

Dog Coat

Back
Using smaller needles and MC, cast on 42 (58, 74) sts.
    Knit 3 rows.

Buttonhole row: K16 (20, 26), k2tog, yo, knit to last 18 (22, 28) sts, yo, k2tog, knit to end of row.
    Knit 3 rows.
    Change to larger needles, and work even in St st and Stripe pat until piece measures 28 (35.5, 43) cm or 11 (14, 17) inches from beg.
    Change to smaller needles and MC, and knit 6 rows.

Belly band
Bind off 14 (18, 24) sts, k14 (18, 22), bind off rem 14 (18, 24) sts.
    Work rem 14 (18, 22) sts in garter st until band measures approximately 9 (12.5, 15)cm or 3½ (5, 6) inches or length needed to reach around belly of dog.
    Bind off all sts.

Back and front edges

*With smaller needles and MC, pick up and knit 44 (58, 71) sts across back edge of coat.

Knit 6 rows.*

Bind off all sts.

Rep from * to * across front edge of coat.

Chest strap

Next row: Bind off 38 (48, 56) sts, knit to end of row.

Continue in garter st until strap measures 15 (20.5, 25.5)cm or 6 (8, 10) inches, or length needed to reach around upper chest comfortably.

Buttonhole row: K2 (3, 4), yo, k2tog, knit to end of row.

Knit 4 rows.

Bind off all sts.

Finishing

Sew 2 buttons on Belly band and 1 button on Chest strap opposite buttonholes. ✦

Strut Your Stuff

Lady will be sitting pretty in her easy lace-knit coat.

DESIGN BY BONNIE FRANZ

EASY

Sizes
Dog's small (medium, large) instructions are given for smallest size, with larger sizes in parentheses. When only 1 number is given, it applies to all sizes.

Finished Measurements
Back width: 33 (40.5, 48.5)cm or 13 (16, 19) inches
Length: 33 (44.5, 56)cm or 13 (17½, 22) inches

Materials
- Plymouth Encore D.K. 75 per cent acrylic/25 per cent wool light weight yarn (137 metres (150 yds)/50g per ball): 2 (2, 3) balls orange #1383
- 3.75mm (size 5) needles or size needed to obtain gauge
- Tapestry needle
- 3 (2-cm/⅞-inch) buttons

Gauge
17 sts and 12 rows (1 full repeat of pat) = 3 x 3.8cm (1½ inches)
To save time, take time to check gauge.

Pattern Stitch
Ridged Old Shale (multiple of 17 sts)
Rows 1-3: Knit.
Row 4 (WS): Purl.
Row 5: *[K2tog] 3 times, [yo, k1] 5 times, yo, [ssk] 3 times; rep from * across.
Row 6: Purl.
Row 7: Knit.
Row 8: Purl.
Row 9: Rep Row 5.
Row 10: Purl.
Rows 11 and 12: Knit.
Rep Rows 1-12 for pat.

Dog Coat

Back
Cast on 68 (85, 102) sts.
Work in Ridged Old Shale until piece measures 30.5 (42, 53.5)cm or 12 (16½, 21) inches from beg.
Bind off 62 (75, 87) sts, knit to end. (6, 10, 15 sts)

Chest band
Work in garter st on rem sts until band measures 15 (20.5, 25.5)cm or 6 (8, 10) inches or length needed to reach around upper chest comfortably.
Bind off.

Side edges
Right edge: Pick up and knit 68 (92, 116) sts. Knit 4 rows. Bind off.
Left edge: Pick up and knit 68 (92, 116) sts. Knit 4 rows.
Bind off 24 (33, 40) sts at beg of next 2 rows. (20, 26, 36 sts)

Belly band
Work even in garter st until band measures 9 (12.5, 15)cm or 3½ (5, 6) inches or length needed to reach around belly of dog.
Bind off all sts.

Finishing
Sew 2 buttons on Belly band and 1 button on Chest band.
Use openings in lace pattern as buttonholes. ✦

Smiley Face Cardigan

Make this cute cardigan for the next baby shower and make everyone smile.

DESIGN BY LORNA MISER

EASY

Size
Infant's 6 months (1 year, 2 years) instructions are given for smallest size, with larger sizes in parentheses. When only 1 number is given, it applies to all sizes.

Finished Measurement
Chest: 51 (56, 61)cm or 20 (22, 24) inches

Materials

- Lion Brand Watercolors 65 per cent acrylic/35 per cent merino wool bulky (chunky) weight yarn (50 metres (55 yds)/ 50g per ball): 3 (4, 5) balls sunset rose #339 (MC), 1 (1, 2) balls bright clouds #398 (CC)
- 6mm (size 10) 61-cm or 24-inch circular needle or size needed to obtain gauge
- Stitch holders
- Stitch markers
- 3 (2-cm/⅞-inch) smiley face buttons

Gauge
12 sts = 10cm/4 inches in St st
To save time, take time to check gauge.

Pattern Notes
Circular needle is used to accommodate large number of sts. Do not join; work back and forth in rows.

Cardigan is knitted in one piece to underarm, then divided for fronts and back. Sleeves are knitted flat, then seamed and sewn to body.

Body
With CC, cast on 60 (66, 72) sts. Knit 3 rows. Change to MC and St st and work even until body measures 15 (18, 20.5)cm or 6 (7, 8) inches from beg, ending with a WS row.

Right Front
Knit across 15 (16, 18) sts, turn.

Continue to work in St st on these sts, dec 1 st by ssk at neck edge [every 4th row] 3 (3, 3) times, then [every RS row] 2 (2, 3) times. (10, 11, 12 sts rem)

Work even until armhole measures 11.5 (12.5, 14)cm or 4½ (5, 5½) inches. Place rem shoulder sts on holder.

Back
Knit across next 30 (34, 36) sts, turn.

Continue to work in St st on these sts until armhole measures same as front to shoulder. Mark centre 10 (12, 12) sts for back neck. Place sts on holder.

Left Front
Knit across rem 15 (16, 18) sts.

Continue to work in St st on these sts, dec 1 st by k2tog at neck edge [every 4th row] 3 (3, 3) times, then [every RS row] 2 (2, 3) times. (10, 11, 12 sts rem)

Work even until armhole measures 11.5 (12.5, 14)cm or 4½ (5, 5½) inches. Place rem shoulder sts on holder.

Join front and back shoulder sts using 3-Needle Bind Off (see page 9). Leave rem sts on holder for back neck.

Sleeves
With CC, cast on 20 (21, 22) sts. Knit 3 rows. Change to MC and St st. Inc 1 st at each edge of first row, then [every 6th row] 3 (4, 5) more times. (28, 31, 34 sts)

Work even until sleeve measures 15 (18, 20.5)cm or 6 (7, 8) inches from beg. Bind off.

Assembly
Sew sleeve seam. Sew sleeve to body.

Front band
Note: *For boys, work buttonholes on left front and sew buttons to right front.*

CONTINUED ON PAGE 152

Making a Wish

Comfort your child in a soft garter stitch jumper.

DESIGN BY SARA LOUISE HARPER

EASY

Size
Child's 2 (4, 6, 8, 10) instructions are given for smallest size, with larger sizes in parentheses. When only 1 number is given, it applies to all sizes.

Finished Measurements
Chest: 61 (66, 71, 76, 8.5)cm or 24 (26, 28, 30, 32) inches
Length: 30.5 (33, 33.5, 38, 40.5)cm or 12 (13, 14, 15, 16) inches

Materials

• Plymouth Baby Rimini 85 per cent acrylic/15 per cent wool super bulky weight yarn (34 metres (38 yds)/50g per ball): 4 (5, 5, 6, 7) balls blue variegated #305 (MC)
• Plymouth Heaven 100 per cent nylon super bulky weight yarn (50 metres (55 yds)/50g per ball): 3 (3, 3, 4, 4) balls lilac #8 (CC)
• 8mm (size 11) straight and 40.5-cm (16-inch) circular needles or size needed to obtain gauge
• Stitch markers

Gauge
9 sts and 16 rows = 10cm/4 inches in garter st
To save time, take time to check gauge.

Stripe Pattern
Rows 1–6: With MC, knit.

Rows 7–10: With CC, knit.
Rep Rows 1–10 for pat.

Back
With MC, cast on 27 (29, 31, 33, 35) sts.
Work even in Stripe pat until back measures 15 (18, 19, 20.5, 20.5)cm or 6 (7, 7½, 8, 8) inches. Mark each end st of last row for underarm.
Continue to work even until armhole measures 15 (15, 16.5, 18, 20.5)cm or 6 (6, 6½, 7, 8) inches above underarm markers, ending with a WS row.
Bind off all sts knitwise.
Mark centre 9 (11, 13, 13, 13) sts for back neck.

Front
Work as for back until front measures 7.5 (7.5, 9, 10, 12.5)cm or 3 (3, 3½, 4, 5) inches above underarm markers, ending with a WS row.

Shape neck
Next row (RS): K11 (11, 11, 12, 13) sts, join 2nd ball of yarn and bind off next 5 (7, 9, 9, 9) sts, knit to end of row.
Working on both sides of neck with separate balls of yarn, [dec 1 st at each neck edge every RS row] twice. (9, 9, 9, 10, 11 sts on each side)

Work even until front measures same as for back above underarm markers.
Bind off all sts knitwise.

Sleeves
With MC cast on 18 sts.
Work even in Stripe pat until sleeve measures 5cm (2 inches) from beg, ending with a WS row.
Inc 1 st each end on next and every following 6th (8th, 8th, 7th, 6th) row 5 (5, 6, 7, 9) times. (28, 28, 30, 32, 36 sts)
Work even until sleeve measures 30.5 (33, 35.5, 38, 40.5)cm or 12 (13, 14, 15, 16) inches in length.
Bind off loosely.
Sew shoulder seams.

Neck Band
With CC and circular needle, pick up and knit 32 (34, 36, 38, 40) sts evenly around neck opening. Pm between first and last st.
[Purl 1 rnd, knit 1 rnd] twice.
Purl 1 rnd.
Bind off loosely knitwise.

Assembly
Sew sleeves to body between underarm markers.
Sew sleeve and side seams. ✦

CONTINUED ON PAGE 152

Team Spirit Jumper

For a first project, knit this jumper in your sports fan's favourite team colours.

DESIGN BY CELESTE PINHEIRO

BEGINNER

Size
Child's 2 (4, 6, 8) instructions are given for smallest size, with larger sizes in parentheses. When only 1 number is given, it applies to all sizes.

Finished Measurements
Chest: 66 (71, 76, 8.5)cm or 26 (28, 30, 32) inches
Total length: 38 (40.5, 43, 46)cm or 15 (16, 17, 18) inches

Materials
• Plymouth Encore Worsted 75 per cent acrylic/25 per cent wool yarn (182 metres (200yds)/100g per ball): 1 (1, 1, 2) ball(s) dark red #9601 (A), 1 ball each medium charcoal #389 (B), light charcoal #194 (C), dark charcoal #520 (D)
• 4mm (size 6) straight and double-pointed needles
• 5mm (size 8) straight and double-pointed needles or size needed to obtain gauge
• Stitch markers
• Tapestry needle

Gauge
16 sts and 23 rows = 10cm/4 inches in St st with larger needles

To save time, take time to check gauge.

Pattern Notes
Lower edges of body and sleeves roll automatically. All measurements are taken with edges unrolled.

Back
With smaller needles and B, cast on 52 (56, 60, 64) sts.

Work in St st for 7 rows changing to larger needles on last WS row.

Work even until back measures 18 (19, 20.5, 21.5)cm or 7 (7½, 8, 8½) inches from beg, ending with a RS row.

Change to A and knit 1 row. Continue in St st until back measures 37 (39, 42, 44.5)cm or 14½ (15½, 16½, 17½) inches from beg, ending with a WS row.

Back neck shaping
Next row (RS): K17 (18, 19, 20), join 2nd ball of yarn and bind off next 18 (20, 22, 24) sts for back neck, knit to end of row. Working on both sides of neck with separate balls of yarn,

dec 1 st at each neck edge. (16, 17, 18, 19 sts on each side of neck)

Work even until back measures 38 (38, 43, 46)cm or 15 (15, 17, 18) inches.

Bind off.

Front
Work as for back until front measures 33 (35.5, 38, 40.5)cm or 13 (14, 15, 16) inches, ending with a WS row.

Front neck shaping
K22 (24, 26, 27), join 2nd ball of yarn and bind off next 8 (8, 8, 10) sts, knit to end of row.

Working on both sides of neck with separate balls of yarn, bind off 3 sts at each neck edge, then 2 sts at each neck edge.

[Dec 1 st at each neck edge every row] 1 (2, 3, 3)

times. (16, 17, 18, 19 sts at each side of neck)

Work even until front measures same as for back.

Bind off.

Neck Band

Sew shoulder seams.

With smaller dpn and B, pick up and knit 52 (56, 60, 64) sts evenly around neck edge.

Join, pm between first and last st.

Purl 1 rnd.

Knit 7 rnds, change to larger dpn and knit 7 more rounds.

Bind off loosely.

Sleeves

With smaller needles and C, cast on 32 sts.

Work in St st for 7 rows changing to larger needles on last WS row.

Inc 1 st at each end of needle on Row 12, then [every following 6th row] 7 (8, 9, 10) times. (48, 50, 52, 54 sts)

At the same time when sleeve measures 10 (12.5, 15, 18)cm or 4 (5, 6, 7) inches, change to D after a RS row.

Next row (WS): Knit.

Continue in St st, inc as before until sleeve measures 25.5 (28, 30.5, 33)cm or 10 (11, 12, 13) inches.

Bind off.

Finishing

Measure down 15 (15.75, 16.5, 17)cm or 6 (6¼, 6½, 6¾) inches on either side of shoulder seam and mark for armhole.

Sew sleeves between markers.

Sew sleeve and underarm seams. ✦

14 (14, 15, 16.5)cm
5½ (5½, 6, 6½)"

5cm
2"

FRONT & BACK

38 (40.5, 43, 46)cm
15 (16, 17, 18)"

33 (35.5, 38, 40.5)cm
13 (14, 15, 16)"

30.5 (31.5, 33, 34)cm
12 (12½, 13, 13½)"

SLEEVE

25.5 (28, 30.5, 33)cm
10 (11, 12, 13)"

20.5cm
8"

Like Father, Like Son

Classic good looks are perfect for a son and the man he looks up to.

DESIGNS BY LORNA MISER

INTERMEDIATE

Size
Child's 6 (8, 10, 12)/Man's small (medium, large, extra-large, 2X-large) instructions are given for smallest size, with larger sizes in parentheses. Child's size is listed first, followed by man's size. When only 1 number is given, it applies to all sizes.

Finished Measurement
Chest: 28 (30, 32, 34) inches/71 (76, 81.5, 86.5)cm/101.5 (112, 122, 132, 142)cm or 40 (44, 48, 52, 56) inches

Materials
- Bernat Solo 72 per cent acrylic/28 per cent polyester bulky weight yarn (79 metres (86yds)/80g per ball): 4 (5, 6, 7)/8 (9, 10, 11, 13) balls tomato #57530/smoke #570400
- 6mm (size 10) 40.5-cm (16-inch) circular needle
- 6.5mm (size 10½) circular and double-pointed needles or size needed to obtain gauge
- Stitch markers
- Stitch holders

Gauge
12 sts = 10cm/4 inches in pat with larger needles

To save time, take time to check gauge.

Pattern Stitch
Basket Weave (multiple of 6 sts)
Rnds 1–4: *K2, p4; rep from * around.
Rnds 5–8: *P3, k2, p1; rep from * around.
    Rep Rnds 1–8 for pat.

Pattern Note
Jumper is knit in the round for a seamless garment. Body and sleeves are knit separately to the underarm, then all three pieces are joined and worked tog for raglan shaping.

Body
With larger circular needle, cast on 84 (90, 96, 102)/120 (132, 144, 156, 168) sts, join without twisting.
    Note: When working next rnd, place markers at beg of rnd and after st #42 (45, 48, 51)/60 (66, 72, 78, 84).
Next rnd: *K1, p1; rep from * around.
    Rep last rnd for 1.75cm (⅔ inches).
    Change to basket weave pat and work even until body

measures approximately 28 (30.5, 33, 38)/38 (40.5, 43, 43, 46)cm or 11 (12, 13, 15)/15 (16, 17, 17, 18) inches from beg, ending with Rnd 4 or 8.
Next rnd: Maintaining pat, *work 3 (3, 3, 4)/5 (5, 6, 6, 6) sts past marker, sl 6 (6, 6, 8)/10 (10, 12, 12, 12) sts just worked onto holder for underarm; rep from *. Cut yarn and set body aside.

Sleeves
With double-pointed needles, cast on 22 (22, 24, 24)/24 (28, 28, 30, 32) sts. Join without twisting. Place markers at beg of rnd and after 2nd st.
Ribbing: *K1, p1; rep from * around.
    Rep this rnd for 4/6.5cm or 1½/2½ inches.
    Change to basket weave pattern, keeping 2 centre marked sts in St st and working incs outside markers. Inc [every 4th row] 6 (7, 8, 8)/12 (12, 14, 16, 17) times. (34, 36, 40, 40/48, 52, 56, 62, 66 sts)
    Work even until sleeve measures approximately 28 (35.5, 38, 43)/46 (48.5, 51, 53.5, 53.5)cm or 11 (14, 15, 17)/18 (19, 20, 21, 21) inches or desired

length to underarm, ending with Rnd 4 or 8.

Last rnd: From 2nd marker, work 2 (2, 2, 3)/4 (4, 5, 5, 5) sts, then sl last 6 (6, 6, 8)/10 (10, 12, 12, 12) sts from RH needle onto a holder for underarm. Cut yarn.

Join for yoke

Attach yarn ready to work across back of jumper. K1 from back, work in basket weave across back to last st, k1 and place marker; k1 from sleeve and work in pat across sleeve to last st, k1 and place marker; k1 from front, work in basket weave across front to last st, k1 and place marker; k1 from sleeve and work in pat across sleeve to last st, k1 and place marker.

Dec rnd: *Ssk, work in pat across back to 2 sts before marker, k2tog, sl marker, ssk, work across sleeve in pat to 2 sts before marker, k2tog, sl marker, ssk, work across front sts to 2 sts before marker, k2tog, sl marker, ssk, work across rem sleeve to 2 sts before marker, k2tog, sl marker. Join and work in rnds.

Next rnd: Work even, keeping 1 st on each side of each marker in St st.

Rep last 2 rnds until yoke measures 10 (11.5, 12.5, 15)/18 (20.5, 23, 24, 24)cm or 4 (4½, 5, 6)/7 (8, 9, 9½, 9½) inches, end by working an even rnd ready to beg front section.

Shape neck

Count number of sts in centre front section and mark centre. Sl 3 (3, 4, 4)/4 (5, 6, 6, 6) sts on each side of centre marker to a holder for centre front neck.

Working back and forth in pat on all rem sts, work raglan dec on RS rows and knit the knit sts, purl the purl sts on WS rows. Dec 1 st at each neck edge [every RS row] 4 (4, 4, 4)/5 (5, 5, 5, 6) times. Continue to work raglan dec until yoke measures 18 (19, 20.5, 23)/25.5 (28, 30.5, 33, 33)cm or 7 (7½, 8, 9)/10 (11, 12, 13, 13) inches.

Neck band

Change to smaller 40.5-cm (16-inch) circular needle. Pick up and knit 6 (7, 9, 9)/9 (9, 9, 10, 10) sts along side front edge, k6 (6, 8, 8)/8 (10, 12, 12, 12) sts from front neck holder, pick up and knit 6 (7, 9, 9)/9 (9, 9, 10, 10) sts along side front edge, work across back neck sts. Work k1, p1 ribbing around neck for approximately 2.5cm (1 inch). Bind off in pat.

Finishing

Weave underarm sts. Block lightly. ✦

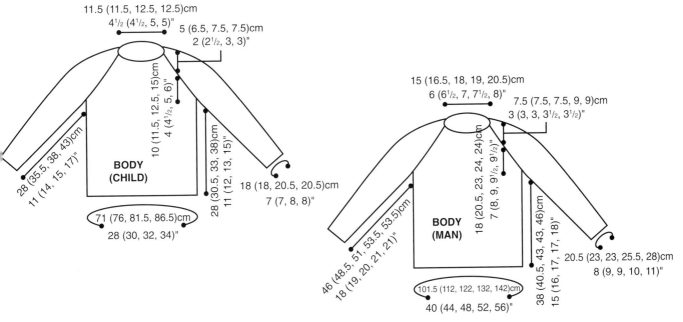

Weekender Jumper

This season-spanning style is fun to knit from sleeve to sleeve.

DESIGN BY ANDRA KNIGHT-BOWMAN

EASY

Sizes

Woman's small (medium, large, extra-large, 2X-large) instructions are given for smallest size, with larger sizes in parentheses. When 1 number is given, it applies to all sizes.

Finished Measurements

Chest: 96.5 (106.5, 117, 127, 137)cm or 38 (42, 46, 50, 54) inches

Materials

- Knitting Fever Inc. Katia Jamaica 100 per cent medium weight cotton yarn (200 metres (219 yds)/100g per ball): 4 (5, 5, 6, 6) balls pinks/ greens #04
- 4mm (size 6) straight and 40.5-cm (16-inch) circular needles or size needed to obtain gauge
- Stitch marker

Gauge

20 sts and 25 rows = 10cm/4 inches in St st
To save time, take time to check gauge.

Special Abbreviation

M1 (Make 1): Inc 1 by inserting LH needle under horizontal strand between st just worked and next st, k1-tbl.

Pattern Note

This jumper is knitted with just one yarn that is self-striping. It's worked in one piece from side to side, starting with left sleeve and ending with right sleeve.

Jumper

Cast on 70 (70, 70, 76, 76) sts. Knit 3 rows, then work in St st for 8 rows.

Inc row: K1, M1, knit to last st, M1, k1.

Continue to work in St st, rep inc row [every 8th row] 4 times. (80, 80, 80, 86, 86 sts)

Work even until sleeve measures 33cm (13 inches) from beg, ending with a WS row.

At beg of next 2 rows, cast on 60 (60, 60, 62, 62) sts. (200, 200, 200, 210, 210 sts)

First 100 (100, 100, 105, 105) sts are back of sweater; place a marker to divide them. Work in St st for an additional 13.25 (15, 18, 20.5, 22.25)cm or 5¼ (6, 7, 8, 8¾) inches, ending with a WS row.

Shape neck

Row 1: Work 100 (100, 100, 105, 105) sts (back), attach a 2nd ball of yarn; bind off next 6 sts, work to end.

Row 2: Purl, working each side separately.

Row 3: Work first 100 (100, 100, 105, 105) sts; bind off 2 sts at beg of neck, work to end.

Row 4: Rep Row 2.

Rows 5–8: [Rep Rows 3 and 4] twice.

Work even until neck opening measures 21.5 (20.5, 20.5, 20.5, 24)cm or 8½ (8, 8, 8, 9½) inches, ending with a RS row.

Next row (WS): Purl to marker, cast on 2 sts at front neck edge; work to end.

Next row: Knit, working each side separately.

Rep [last 2 rows] twice.

Next row: Purl to marker, cast on 6 sts at front neck edge, work to end.

Next row: Knit across, joining sts at neck and dropping 2nd ball of yarn. (200, 200, 200, 210, 210 sts)

Work even until neck opening measures 19 (20.5, 20.5, 20.5, 21.5)cm or 7½ (8, 8, 8, 8½) inches.

Sleeve

Bind off 60 (60, 60, 62, 62) sts at beg of next 2 rows. (80, 80, 80, 86, 86 sts)

CONTINUED ON PAGE 153

Checks & Stripes Twin Set

Take a colourful tank top, add a vivid cardigan and your wardrobe possibilities become greatly expanded.

DESIGN BY KENNITA TULLY

EASY

Size
Woman's small (medium, large, extra-large) instructions are given for smallest size, with larger sizes in parentheses. When only 1 number is given, it applies to all sizes.

Finished Measurements
Tank
Chest: 91.5 (100, 106.5, 114.5)cm or 36 (39½, 42, 45) inches
Length: 48.5 (51, 53.5, 56)cm or 19 (20, 21, 22) inches

Cardigan
Chest: 96.5 (106.5, 117, 127)cm or 38 (42, 46, 50) inches
Length: 51 (53.5, 56, 58.5)cm or 20 (21, 22, 23) inches

Materials
Tank
- Brown Sheep Cotton Fleece 80 per cent Prima cotton/20 per cent Merino wool worsted weight yarn (197 metres(215 yds)/100g per skein): 3 (3, 4, 4) skeins tea rose #CW210
- 3.75mm (size 5) 40.5-cm (16-inch) circular needle

- 4mm (size 6) needles or size needed to obtain gauge
- Stitch markers

Cardigan
- Brown Sheep Cotton Fine 80 per cent Prima cotton/20 per cent Merino wool fingering weight yarn (203 metres (222 yds)/50g per ball): 5 (5, 6, 6) balls each cotton ball #CW100, tea rose #CW210, blue paradise #CW765
- 4mm (size 6) needles
- 5mm (size 8) needles or size needed to obtain gauge
- Stitch markers
- 1 (2.5-cm/1-inch) button

Gauge
Tank
18 sts and 28 rows = 10cm/4 inches in Wide Shadow Rib pat with larger needles

Cardigan
18 sts and 28 rows = 10cm/4 inches in Slip Stitch Mesh pat with larger needles
To save time, take time to check gauge.

Pattern Stitches
A. Narrow Shadow Rib
(multiple of 3 sts + 2)
Row 1 (RS): P2, *k1-tbl, p2; rep from * across.
Row 2: Knit.
Rep Rows 1 and 2 for pat.

B. Wide Shadow Rib
(multiple of 6 sts + 5)
Row 1 (RS): P5, *k1-tbl, p5; rep from * across.
Row 2: Knit.
Rep Rows 1 and 2 for pat.

C. Twisted Rib
(multiple of 3 sts)
All rnds: *K1-tbl, p2; rep from * around.

D. Slip Stitch Mesh
Row 1 (RS): Purl.
Row 2: Knit.
Row 3: K2, *sl 1 wyib, k1; rep from * to last 2 sts, k2.
Row 4: K2, *sl 1 wyif, k1; rep from * to last 2 sts, k2.
Row 5: K2, *yo, k2tog; rep from * to last 2 sts, k2.
Row 6: Purl.
Rep Rows 1–6 for pat.

Pattern Note
Hold 1 strand of each colour tog for entire cardigan.

Shadow Rib Tank

Back
With larger needles, cast on 83 (89, 95, 101) sts.

Work even in Narrow Shadow Rib for 4 rows.

Change to Wide Shadow Rib and work even until back measures 30.5 (31, 33, 34)cm or 12 (12½, 13, 13½) inches, ending with a WS row.

Shape armholes
Next 2 rows: Bind off 6 (7, 7, 7) sts, work to end of row. (71, 75, 81, 87 sts)
Dec row: Ssk, work in pat to last 2 sts, k2tog.

Work dec row [every other row] 4 (4, 5, 5) times, then [every

4th row] twice. (59, 63, 67, 73 sts)

Work even until armhole measures 18 (19, 20.5, 21.5)cm or 7 (7½, 8, 8½) inches, ending with a WS row.

Shape shoulders and neck
Next row (RS): Bind off 6 (5, 6, 7) sts, work across next 10 (12, 12, 12) sts, k2tog, place rem sts on holder.

[Bind off 5 (6, 6, 6) sts at arm edge] twice.

Sl sts from holder to needle. With RS facing, join yarn at next st.

Bind off 25 (27, 29, 33) sts, ssk, work to end of row.

Bind off at arm edge 6 (5, 6, 7) sts once, then 5 (6, 6, 6) sts twice.

Front
Work as for back until armhole measures 10 (11.5, 12.5, 14)cm or 4 (4½, 5, 5½) inches, ending with a WS row.

Shape neck
Work across 22 (23, 24, 26) sts, attach 2nd ball of yarn. Bind off next 15 (17, 19, 21) sts for front neck, work to end of row.

Working on both sides of neck with separate balls of yarn, bind off 2 sts at each neck edge.

Dec 1 st at each neck edge [every other row] 2 (2, 2, 3) times, then [every 4th row] twice. (16, 17, 18, 19 sts)

Work even until armhole measures same as back.

Shape shoulders
Bind off at each arm edge 6 (5,

6, 7) sts once, then 5 (6, 6, 6) sts twice.

Sew shoulder and side seams.

Armbands
Beg at underarm with smaller circular needle, pick up and knit 90 (93, 99, 102) sts around armhole. Join, pm between first and last st.

Work in Twisted Rib pat for 2 rnds.

Bind off in pat.

Neck Band
Beg at right shoulder with smaller circular needle, pick up and knit 33 (34, 38, 41) sts along back neck to left shoulder, 18 (18, 18, 20) sts along left side neck, 15 (17, 19, 21) sts along front neck and 18 (18, 18, 20) sts along right side of neck. (84, 87, 93, 102 sts)

Work in Twisted Rib pat for 2 rnds.

Bind off in pat.

Slip Stitch Mesh Cardigan

Back
With larger needles, cast on 86 (94, 106, 114) sts.

Work even in Slip Stitch Mesh pat until back measures 30.5 (31, 33, 34)cm or 12 (12½, 13, 13½) inches.

Mark each end st of last row for underarm.

Work even until back measures approximately 51 (53.5, 56, 58.5)cm or 20 (21, 22, 23) inches, ending with Row 2 of pat.

Bind off.

Front

(make both alike)

With larger needles, cast on 42 (46, 52, 56) sts.

Work as for back.

Sleeves

With larger needles, cast on 36 (40, 44, 48) sts.

Working in Slip Stitch Mesh pat, inc 1 st each end [every 6th row] 3 times, then [every 8th row] 14 times. (72, 76, 80, 84 sts)

Work even until sleeve measures approximately 51cm (20 inches), ending with Row 2 of pat.

Bind off.

Assembly

Pm for shoulder 15 (16.5, 19, 21.5)cm or 6 (6½, 7½, 8½) inches from armhole on all pieces.

Sew shoulder seams.

Sew sleeves to body between underarm markers.

Sew sleeve and side seams.

Button Band

Beg at top edge with smaller needles and RS facing, pick up and purl [2 sts for every 3 rows] 12 (12, 14, 14) times, pm, then pick up and knit at the same ratio to lower edge. Record number of picked-up sts after marker.

Knit 4 rows.

Bind off.

Mark top 24 (24, 28, 28) sts for collar.

Buttonhole Band

Beg at lower edge with smaller needles and RS facing, working at a 2:3 ratio as before, pick up and knit recorded number of sts for button band, pm, pick up and purl 24 (24, 28, 28) sts to top edge.

Knit 1 row.

Buttonhole row: Knit to 4 sts before marker, bind off next 4 sts, knit to end of row.

Knit 2 more rows, casting on 4 sts over previous bound-off area.

Bind off.

Mark top 24 (24, 28, 28) sts for collar.

Collar Edging

With WS facing, pick up and knit 18 (19, 21, 21) sts across left front to shoulder, pick up and purl 33 (35, 37, 37) sts across back neck, pick up and knit 18 (19, 21, 21) sts across right front. (69, 73, 79, 79 sts)

Knit 4 rows.

Bind off.

Turn collar back at marked st. Tack collar point to front of cardigan.

Sew on button. ◆

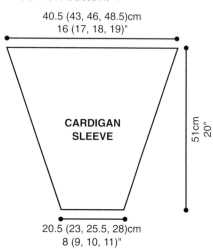

40.5 (43, 46, 48.5)cm
16 (17, 18, 19)"

CARDIGAN SLEEVE

51cm
20"

20.5 (23, 25.5, 28)cm
8 (9, 10, 11)"

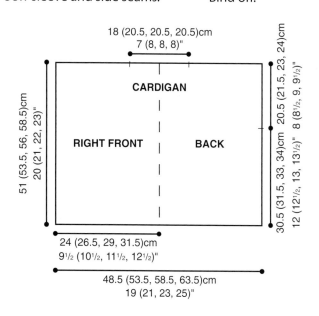

18 (20.5, 20.5, 20.5)cm
7 (8, 8, 8)"

CARDIGAN

RIGHT FRONT   BACK

51 (53.5, 56, 58.5)cm
20 (21, 22, 23)"

20.5 (21.5, 23, 24)cm
8 (8½, 9, 9½)"

30.5 (31.5, 33, 34)cm
12 (12½, 13, 13½)"

24 (26.5, 29, 31.5)cm
9½ (10½, 11½, 12½)"

48.5 (53.5, 58.5, 63.5)cm
19 (21, 23, 25)"

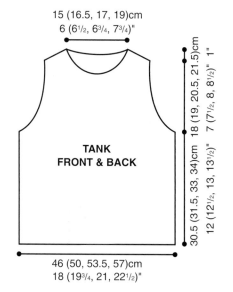

15 (16.5, 17, 19)cm
6 (6½, 6¾, 7¾)"

TANK
FRONT & BACK

18 (19, 20.5, 21.5)cm
7 (7½, 8, 8½)"

1"

30.5 (31.5, 33, 34)cm
12 (12½, 13, 13½)"

46 (50, 53.5, 57)cm
18 (19¾, 21, 22½)"

Peachy Party Cardigan

It's easy to have fun making and then wearing this lovely cardigan.

DESIGN BY CIA ABBOTT BULLEMER

EASY

Sizes
Woman's small (medium, large) instructions are given for smallest size, with larger sizes in parentheses. When only 1 number is given it applies to all sizes.

Finished Measurements
Chest: 89 (96.5, 101.5)cm or 35 (38, 40) inches
Length: 49.5 (53.5, 56)cm or 19½ (21, 22) inches

Materials
- Plymouth Platinum 20 per cent angora/30 per cent nylon/50 per cent rayon medium weight yarn (91 metres (99 yds)/50g per ball): 4 (5, 6) balls peach #6 (A) **[4 MEDIUM]**
- Plymouth Margarita 78 per cent nylon/22 per cent microtacted bulky weight yarn (80 metres (88 yds)/50g per ball): 2 (3, 4) balls peach medley #3527 (B) **[5 BULKY]**
- Plymouth Daiquiri 70 per cent nylon/30 per cent cotton medium weight yarn (85 metres (93 yds)/50g per ball): 2 (3, 4) balls peach blend #3527 (C) **[4 MEDIUM]**
- 6mm (size 10) needles
- 7mm (size 10½) needles
- Stitch holders
- 6mm (size J/10) crochet hook

Gauge
16 sts = 10cm/4 inches in St st with A and larger needles
14 sts = 10cm/4 inches in Lattice St pat with B and smaller needles
11 sts = 10cm/4 inches in Stockinette Ridges pat with C and larger needles
To save time, take time to check gauge.

Pattern Stitches
A. Lattice
(even number of sts)
Row 1: K1, *k2tog, yo; rep from * to last st, end k1.
Rep Row 1 for pat.

B. Stockinette Ridge
(any number of sts)
Row 1 (RS): Knit across.
Row 2: Purl across.
Rows 3 and 4: Knit across.
Rep Rows 1–4 for pat.

Back
With B and smaller needles, cast on 68 (76, 80) sts. Work in Lattice pat until back measures 10 (11.5, 12.5)cm or 4 (4½, 5) inches.
Change to A and larger needles and work in St st until back measures 30.5 (33, 38)cm or 12 (13, 15) inches.

Shape armhole
Bind off 3 (4, 5) sts at beg of next 2 rows. (62, 68, 70 sts rem)
Continue to work in St st until back measures 49.5 (53.5, 56)cm or 19½ (21, 23) inches, ending with a WS row.

Shape shoulders
K21 (24, 25), place sts on a holder; bind off centre 20 sts; k21 (24, 25) and place sts on a holder.

Left Front
With B and smaller needles, cast on 34 (38, 40) sts. Work in Lattice pat until front measures 10 (11.5, 12.5)cm or 4 (4½, 5) inches.
Change to A and larger needles and work in St st until front measures 23 (25.5, 30.5)cm or 9 (10, 12) inches, ending with a RS row.

Shape neck & armhole

At beg of WS rows, bind off 1 st [every 8th row] 4 times, then [every 6th row] 6 times. *At the same time,* when front measures same as back to underarm, bind off at beg of RS row [3 (4, 5) sts] once.

Continue to work in St st until front measures 49.5 (53.5, 58.5)cm or 19½ (21, 23) inches. Place rem 21 (24, 25) sts on a holder.

Right Front

Work as for left front until front measures 23 (25.5, 30.5)cm or 9 (10, 12) inches, ending with a WS row.

Shape neck

At beg of RS rows, bind off 1 st [every 8th row] 4 times, then [every 6th row] 6 times. *At the same time,* when front measures same as back to underarm, bind off at beg of WS row [3 (4, 5) sts] once.

Continue to work in St st until front measures 49.5 (53.5, 58.5)cm or 19½ (21, 23) inches. Place rem 21 (24, 25) sts on a holder.

Bind off front and back shoulders tog, using 3-needle bind off.

Sleeves

With C and larger needles, RS facing, pick up and knit 64 (72, 72) sts along armhole edge of front and back.

Work in Stockinette Ridge pat, dec 1 st at each edge [every 4th row] 12 (13, 13) times. (40, 46, 46 sts rem)

Continue to work in established pat until sleeve measures 23 (25.5, 30.5)cm or 9 (10, 11) inches, ending with a WS row. With same size needles, change to A, knit 4 rows (garter st).

Change to smaller needles and B, and work in Lattice pat until sleeve measures 35.5 (38, 40.5)cm or 14 (15, 16) inches, or desired length. Bind off all sts.

Assembly

Lay cardigan flat and cover with a damp towel. Using a dry iron set on acrylic setting, lightly press each section. Lay flat until dry. Once pieces are dry, sew side and sleeve seams.

Ties and Edging

Note: *If not familiar with single crochet st (sc), refer to page 9.*

With crochet hook and B, crochet a chain 12.5cm (5 inches) long, do not cut yarn. With chain still attached and RS facing, beg at right front edge just above B border, work sc up front at a rate of approximately 1 sc in every 2nd row and 1 sc for every st, around neck and down left front edge to beg of B border; work a 12.5-cm (5-inch) chain to match right side. Fasten off. ◆

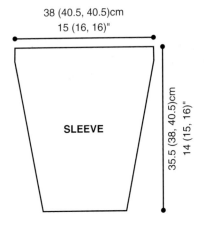

38 (40.5, 40.5)cm
15 (16, 16)"

SLEEVE

35.5 (38, 40.5)cm
14 (15, 16)"

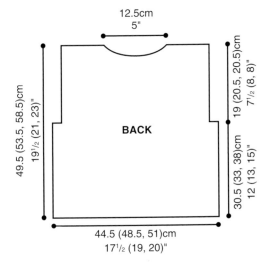

12.5cm
5"

BACK

49.5 (53.5, 58.5)cm
19½ (21, 23)"

19 (20.5, 20.5)cm
7½ (8, 8)"

30.5 (33, 38)cm
12 (13, 15)"

44.5 (48.5, 51)cm
17½ (19, 20)"

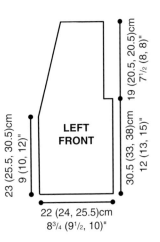

LEFT FRONT

23 (25.5, 30.5)cm
9 (10, 12)"

19 (20.5, 20.5)cm
7½ (8, 8)"

30.5 (33, 38)cm
12 (13, 15)"

22 (24, 25.5)cm
8¾ (9½, 10)"

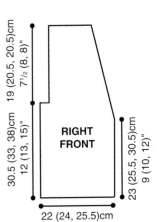

RIGHT FRONT

19 (20.5, 20.5)cm
7½ (8, 8)"

30.5 (33, 38)cm
12 (13, 15)"

23 (25.5, 30.5)cm
9 (10, 12)"

22 (24, 25.5)cm
8¾ (9½, 10)"

Sheer Stripings Tunic

This mostly mohair and totally luscious jumper will pair up with everything from denim to silk.

DESIGN BY SCARLET TAYLOR

EASY

Size
Woman's small (medium, large, extra-large, 2X-large) instructions are given for smallest size, with larger sizes in parentheses. When only 1 number is given, it applies to all sizes.

Finished Measurements
Chest: 95 (106.5, 118, 127, 137)cm or 37½ (42, 46½, 50, 54) inches
Length: 63.5 (66, 66, 67, 68.5)cm or 25 (26, 26, 26½, 27) inches

Materials
• Plymouth Yesterday 80 per cent mohair/15 per cent wool bulky weight yarn (101 metres (110 yds)/50g per ball): 6 (7, 7, 8, 8) balls #1607 (self-striping)
• 9mm (size 13) needles or size needed to obtain gauge
• 6.5mm (size K/10½) crochet hook
• 9mm (size M/13) crochet hook

Gauge
10½ sts and 14 rows = 10cm/4 inches in St st
To save time, take time to check gauge.

Special Abbreviation
M1 (Make 1): Inc 1 by inserting LH needle under horizontal strand between st just worked and next st, k1-tbl.

Back
Cast on 49 (55, 61, 65, 71) sts.
Beg with a RS row, work even in St st until back measures approximately 40.5 (42, 40.5, 40.5, 42)cm or 16 (16½, 16, 16, 16½) inches from beg, ending with a WS row.

Shape armholes
Bind off 2 sts at beg of next 2 (2, 4, 6, 8) rows, then dec 1 st at each edge [every RS row] 2 (4, 3, 2, 1) times. (41, 43, 47, 49, 53 sts)
Continue to work even in St st until armhole measures 18 (19, 20.5, 21.5, 21.5)cm or 7 (7½, 8, 8½, 8½) inches from beg, ending with a WS row.

Shape back neck
Work across first 10 (10, 12, 13, 15) sts; join 2nd ball of yarn and bind off centre 21 (23, 23, 23, 23) sts for back neck, continue in St st across rem 10 (10, 12, 13, 15) sts.
Working both sides at once with separate balls, [dec 1 st at each neck edge] once. (9, 9, 11, 12, 14 sts rem on each side)

Continue to work even until armhole measures 20.5 (21.5, 23, 24, 24)cm or 8 (8½, 9, 9½, 9½) inches from beg, ending with a WS row.

Shape shoulders
Bind off at beg of row [5 (5, 6, 6, 7) sts] twice, then [4 (4, 5, 6, 7) sts] twice.

Front
Work as for back until armhole measures 15 (16.5, 18, 19, 19)cm or 6 (6½, 7, 7½, 7½) inches from underarm, ending with a WS row.

Shape front neck
Continuing in St st, work across first 16 (17, 19, 20, 22) sts; join 2nd ball of yarn and bind off centre 9 sts for front neck, continue across rem 16 (17, 19, 20, 22) sts.
Working both sides at once with separate balls, bind off at each neck edge [4 sts] once, [2 (3, 3, 3, 3) sts] once, then dec 1 st at each neck edge. (9, 9, 11, 12, 14 sts rem on each side)
Continue to work even, if necessary, until armhole measures same as back to

shoulders, ending with a WS row.

Shape shoulders as for back.

Sleeves

Cast on 26 (27, 29, 30, 30) sts.

Beg with a RS row, work even in St st for 4 rows.

Beg on next row and working [M1] 1 st in from edge, inc 1 st at each edge [every 4th row] 0 (4, 3, 5, 5) times, then [every 6th row] 8 (5, 6, 5, 5) times. (42, 45, 47, 50, 50 sts)

Work even until sleeve measures approximately 39 (38, 38.5, 40, 40)cm or 15½ (15, 15¼, 15¾, 15¾) inches from beg, ending with a WS row.

Shape cap

Bind off 2 sts at beg of next 2 (2, 4, 6, 8) rows, then dec 1 st at each edge [every RS row] 2 (4, 3, 2, 1) times. Bind off rem 34 (33, 33, 34, 32) sts.

Assembly

Sew shoulder seams. Set in sleeves.

Sew sleeve seams. Sew side seams, leaving lower 11.5cm (4½ inches) open for slits.

Crochet Edges
Neck edge

With smaller crochet hook and RS facing, attach yarn with a sl st at neck edge of left shoulder seam, and ch 1. Work 1 rnd sc evenly around, working dec sc into each inside corner of neckline. Join with a sl st to first sc. Fasten off.

Bottom edge

With larger crochet hook and RS facing, attach yarn with a sl st to lower left side seam and ch 1. Work 1 rnd sc evenly around edge, working 3 sc into each corner. Join with a sl st to first sc. Fasten off.

Rep for side slits and sleeves. ◆

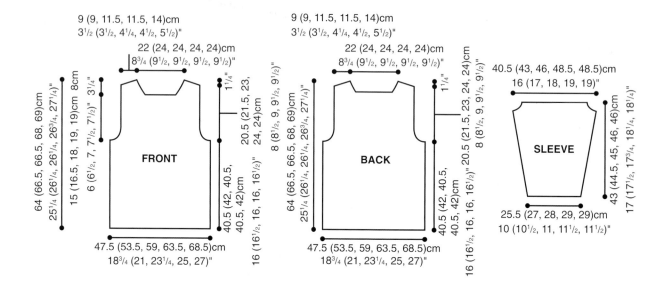

In My Denims

Relax while you knit this easy jumper—perfect for a first jumper or gift.

DESIGN BY SHARI HAUX

EASY

Size
Woman's small (medium, large, extra-large, 2X-large) instructions are given for smallest size, with larger sizes in parentheses. When only 1 number is given, it applies to all sizes.

Finished Measurement
Chest: 91.5 (101.5, 112, 122, 132)cm or 36 (40, 44, 48, 52) inches

Materials
- South West Trading Co. Karaoke 50 per cent soy silk/50 per cent wool worsted weight yarn (101 metres (110 yds)/50g per ball): 10 (11, 12, 13, 15) balls bluezzzz #283
- 4.5mm (size 7) straight and 40.5-cm (16-inch) circular needles
- 5mm (size 8) straight and 40.5-cm (16-inch) circular needles or size needed to obtain gauge
- Stitch holders
- Stitch markers

Gauge
18 sts and 26 rows = 10cm/4 inches in St st with larger needles

To save time, take time to check gauge.

Back
With smaller needles, cast on 81 (91, 99, 107, 117) sts and work 8 rows of St st.
   Change to larger needles.
Rows 1–14: Beg with a RS row, work in St st.
Row 15: Knit across.
Rows 16, 18 and 19: Knit across.
Row 17: *K2 tog, yo; rep from * to last st, end k1.
Row 20: Purl across.
   Rep Rows 1–20 until back measures approximately 59.5 (61, 61, 63.5, 68.5)cm or 23½ (24, 24, 25, 27) inches, ending with a WS St st row.

Shape neck
Knit across 27 (32, 36, 39, 44) sts, bind off centre 27 (27, 27, 29, 29) sts, knit to end of row. Slip shoulder sts to holders.

Front
Work as for back until front measures 26 (26, 26, 28, 28) rows less than back.

Shape neck
Maintaining pat, work across 30

(35, 39, 42, 47) sts; attach 2nd ball of yarn and bind off centre 21 (21, 21, 23, 23) sts, complete row.
   Working both sides with separate balls of yarn, continue in pat, dec 1 st at each neck edge [every other row] 3 times. (27, 32, 36, 39, 44 sts on each shoulder)
   Work even until front measures same as back to shoulder.
   Bind off front and back shoulders, using 3-Needle Bind Off, page 9.

Neck band
Beg at left shoulder seam with smaller circular needle and RS facing, pick up and knit 20 (20,

20, 22, 24) sts along left front neck edge, 21 (21, 21, 23, 23) sts across front neck, 20 (20, 20, 22, 24) sts along right front neck edge, 27 (27, 27, 29, 29) sts across back neck. (88, 88, 88, 96, 100 sts)

Join and work 10 rnds of St st, then change to larger needle and work 4 more rnds of St st. Bind off all sts.

Sleeves

Note: *In order for sleeve to match front and back, measure desired sleeve length on jumper back to determine starting row of pat at sleeve top.*

With RS facing, place marker 25.5 (25.5, 26.5, 26.5, 28)cm or 10 (10, 10½, 10½, 11) inches below shoulder seam on front and back. With larger needles, pick up and knit 91 (91, 93, 93, 95) sts between markers.

Beg pat as determined

above, work as for back, *at the same time,* beg on 13th row, dec 1 st at each end of row every 4th row until 45 (45, 47, 47, 49) sts rem, then work even until sleeve measures 43 (43, 44.5, 44.5)cm or 17 (17, 17½, 17½, 19) inches. Change to smaller needles and work 8 rows of St st. Bind off all sts.

Assembly

Sew sleeve and side seams. ◆

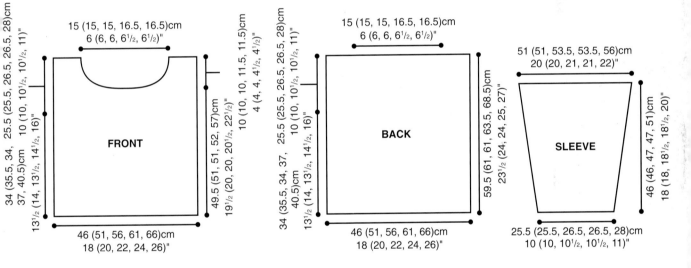

Hot Chocolate Jumper

The soft, cuddly feel and warm colours will remind you of hot milk, marshmallows and chocolate. This jumper is so inviting, you'll want to wear it again and again.

DESIGN BY POSEY SALEM

EASY

Sizes
Woman's small (medium, large, extra-large, 2X-large) instructions are given for smallest size, with larger sizes in parentheses. When only 1 number is given, it applies to all sizes.

Finished Measurements
Chest: 86.5 (96.5, 106.5, 117, 127)cm or 34 (38, 42, 46, 50) inches
Length: 56 (57, 59, 61, 63.5)cm or 22 (22½, 23¼, 24, 25) inches

Materials
- N.Y. Yarns 50 per cent acrylic/47 per cent polyester bulky worsted weight yarn (96 metres (105 yds)/50g per ball): 11 (13, 14, 16, 18) balls brown/beige/white #1
- 5mm (size 8) straight and 40.5-cm (16-inch) circular needles
- 5.5mm (size 9) straight and 40.5-cm (16-inch) circular needles or size needed to obtain gauge
- Stitch marker
- Stitch holders

Gauge
16 sts and 24 rows = 10cm/4 inches in St st with larger needles
To save time, take time to check gauge.

Pattern Stitch
K2, P2 Rib
(multiple of 4 sts)
Row 1 (WS): *P2, k2; rep from * across.
Row 2: *K2, p2; rep from * across.
Rep Rows 1 and 2 for pat.
Note: To work in rnds, rep Row 2 throughout.

Pattern Note
Jumper is designed to be close-fitting; the knit fabric has a lot of elasticity.

Back
With smaller needles, cast on 68 (76, 84, 92, 100) sts and work in K2, P2 Rib for 4cm (1½ inches), ending with a WS row.
Change to larger needles and work in St st until back measures 35.5 (35.5, 37, 38, 39)cm or 14 (14, 14½, 15, 15½) inches from beg, ending with a WS row.

Shape armhole
At beg of next 2 rows, bind off 5 (7, 8, 8, 9) sts. (58, 62, 68, 76, 82 sts)
Work even until back measures approximately 56 (57, 59, 61, 63.5)cm or 22 (22½, 23¼, 24, 25) inches from beg, ending with a WS row.

Shape shoulders
At beg of next row, bind off 17 (18, 20, 23, 25) sts, cut yarn. Sl next 24 (26, 28, 30, 32) sts to a holder.
Attach yarn to next st and bind off rem 17 (18, 20, 23, 25) sts.

Front
Work as for back until front measures 47 (48.5, 50, 52, 54.5)cm or 18½ (19, 19¾, 20½, 21½) inches, ending with a WS row.

Shape neck
K22 (24, 27, 30, 33); sl next 14 (14, 14, 16, 16) sts to a holder;

attach 2nd ball of yarn, k22 (24, 27, 30, 33).

Working both sides at once with separate balls of yarn, at each neck edge [bind off 3 sts] 1 (0, 0, 0, 1) time, then [bind off 2 sts] 1 (2, 2, 2, 1) time(s).

Dec 1 st at each neck edge [every RS row] 0 (2, 3, 3, 3) times by knitting to within 3 sts of neck, k2tog, k1; on 2nd side, k1, ssk, knit to end of row. (17, 18, 20, 23, 25 sts rem for each shoulder)

Work even until front measures same as back. Bind off all sts.

Sleeves

With smaller needles, cast on 30 (32, 36, 38, 44) sts. Beg K2, P2 Rib and work even for 10cm (4 inches), ending with a WS row.

Change to larger needles and beg St st; inc 1 st at each side by knitting into the front and back of first and last st [every 6th row] 17 (18, 0, 0, 0) times then [every 7th row] 0 (0, 17, 17, 16) times. (64, 68, 70, 72, 76 sts)

Work even until sleeve measures 53.5 (58.5, 63.5, 64.5, 66)cm or 21 (23, 25, 25½, 26) inches. Bind off all sts.

Assembly

Sew shoulder seams. Sew sleeves to shoulder edge. Sew sleeve and side seams.

Neck

With smaller circular needle, RS facing, pick up and knit 76 (76, 80, 84, 84) sts evenly around neck edge, including sts from holders. Place marker and join to work K2, P2 Rib in rnds until neck measures 10cm (4 inches). Change to larger circular needle and continue in established rib until turtleneck measures 23cm (9 inches) from beg. Bind off all sts very loosely in pat. ◆

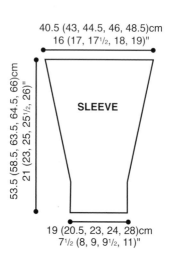

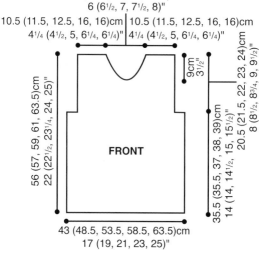

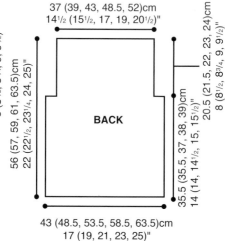

In the Holiday Spirit

Whether dressed up or down, this bright bouclé cardigan is a sensational look.

DESIGN BY KENNITA TULLY

EASY

Size
Woman's small (medium, large, extra-large, 2X-large) instructions are given for smallest size, with larger sizes in parentheses. When only 1 number is given, it applies to all sizes.

Finished Measurements
Chest: 91.5 (101.5, 112, 122, 133)cm or 36 (40, 44, 48, 52½) inches
Length: 56 (58.5, 61, 63.5, 66)cm or 22 (23, 24, 25, 26) inches

Materials
- Knit One, Crochet Too Petite Boucle 58 per cent nylon/21 per cent kid mohair/21 per cent merino worsted weight boucle yarn (75 metres (82 yds)/50g per ball): 9 (10, 11, 12, 14) balls carnation #255
- 5.5mm (size 9) needles or size needed to obtain gauge
- 6mm (size J/10) crochet hook (for trim)
- 3 (2-cm/¾-inch) buttons

4 MEDIUM

Gauge
11½ sts and 18 rows = 10cm/4 inches in St st (steamed) See Pattern Notes
To save time, take time to check gauge.

Special Abbreviation
M1 (Make 1): Inc by making a backward lp over RH needle.

Pattern Notes
Inc are worked 2 sts in from edge, using M1 technique.
Gauge should be measured after blocking with steam. Steaming will spread sts.

Back
Cast on 53 (58, 64, 70, 76) sts and work in St st until back measures approximately 33 (34, 35.5, 37, 38)cm or 13 (13½, 14, 14½, 15) inches.

Shape armholes
Bind off 4 (5, 6, 7, 8) sts at beg of next 2 rows, then dec 1 st at each edge [alternately every 4th row, then every 2nd row] 4 (4, 3, 3, 3) times, then [every other row] 7 (8, 12, 13, 14) times, (work even, if necessary) until armhole measures approximately 23 (24, 25.5, 26.5, 28)cm or 9 (9½, 10, 10½, 11) inches. (15, 16, 16, 18, 20 sts)
Bind off all sts on next RS row.

Right Front
Cast on 28 (31, 34, 37, 40) sts and work in St st until front measures

same as back to underarm, ending with a RS row.

Shape armhole
Bind off 4 (5, 6, 7, 8) sts at beg of next row, then dec 1 st at armhole edge [alternately every 4th row, then every 2nd row] 4 (4, 3, 3, 3) times, then [every other row] 7 (8, 12, 13, 14) times, and *at the same time,* shape collar.

Shape collar
Inc 1 st at neck edge on same row as beg of armhole shaping,

then [every 8th row] 4 more times. (14, 15, 15, 16, 17 sts)

When front measures same as back to shoulder, bind off all sts.

Left Front

Work as for right front to underarm, ending with a WS row.

Shape armhole

Bind off 4 (5, 6, 7, 8) sts at beg of next row, then dec 1 st at armhole edge [alternately every 4th row, then every 2nd row] 4 (4, 3, 3, 3) times, then [every other row] 7 (8, 12, 13, 14) times, and *at the same time,* shape collar.

Shape collar

Inc 1 st at neck edge on same row as beg of armhole shaping, then [every 8th row] 4 more times. (14, 15, 15, 16, 17 sts)

When front measures same as back to shoulder, bind off all sts.

Sleeves

Cast on 22 (24, 26, 28, 30) sts and

work as for back, inc 1 st at each side on 5th row, then [every 6th row] 11 more times. (46, 48, 50, 52, 54 sts)

Work even until sleeve measures approximately 42.5cm (16¾ inches).

Shape sleeve cap

Bind off 4 (5, 6, 7, 8) sts at beg of next 2 rows, then dec 1 st at each edge [alternately every 4th row, then every 2nd row] 4 (5, 6, 7, 7) times, then [every 2nd (2nd, 2nd, 2nd, 4th) row] 7 (5, 3, 1, 1) times. Bind off rem 8 sts.

Assembly

Block all pieces to measurements. Sew sleeves to back and fronts. Sew sleeve and side seams.

Trim

Note: If not familiar with sc (single crochet) and ch (chain) sts refer to page 9.

Mark placement of 3 buttonholes approximately 5cm (2 inches) apart with top

buttonhole beg 2.5cm (1 inch) above armhole shaping. With RS facing and crochet hook, work a sc edging along bottom back edge, right front edge, making buttonholes at each marker by ch 2, then continuing with sc trim until next buttonhole and rep for each buttonhole along right centre front, back neck, left centre front and left front edge. Rep trim for cuffs. Sew buttons opposite lps. ◆

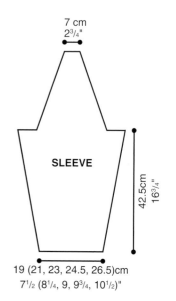

7 cm
2¾"

SLEEVE

42.5cm
16¾"

19 (21, 23, 24.5, 26.5)cm
7½ (8¼, 9, 9¾, 10½)"

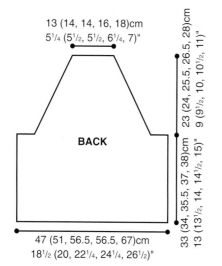

13 (14, 14, 16, 18)cm
5¼ (5½, 5½, 6¼, 7)"

BACK

23 (24, 25.5, 26.5, 28)cm
9 (9½, 10, 10½, 11)"

33 (34, 35.5, 37, 38)cm
13 (13½, 14, 14½, 15)"

47 (51, 56.5, 56.5, 67)cm
18½ (20, 22¼, 24¼, 26½)"

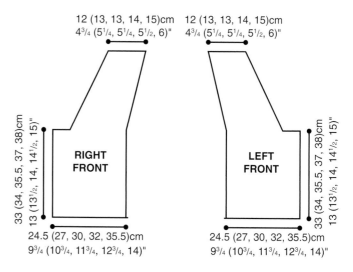

12 (13, 13, 14, 15)cm
4¾ (5¼, 5¼, 5½, 6)"

RIGHT FRONT

33 (34, 35.5, 37, 38)cm
13 (13½, 14, 14½, 15)"

24.5 (27, 30, 32, 35.5)cm
9¾ (10¾, 11¾, 12¾, 14)"

12 (13, 13, 14, 15)cm
4¾ (5¼, 5¼, 5½, 6)"

LEFT FRONT

33 (34, 35.5, 37, 38)cm
13 (13½, 14, 14½, 15)"

24.5 (27, 30, 32, 35.5)cm
9¾ (10¾, 11¾, 12¾, 14)"

Blazer Style Cardigan

A jacket that is timeless and elegant—dress it up or dress it down, it will always look great!

DESIGN BY SARA LOUISE HARPER

INTERMEDIATE

Size

Woman's small (medium, large, extra-large, 2X-large, 3X-large) instructions are given for smallest size, with larger sizes in parentheses. When only 1 number is given, it applies to all sizes.

Finished Measurements

Chest: 96.5 (106.5, 117, 127, 137, 147)cm or 38 (42, 46, 50, 54, 58) inches
Length: 62 (64.5, 66, 67, 70, 71)cm or 24½ (25½, 26, 26½, 27½, 28) inches

Materials

• Patons Shetland Chunky 75 per cent acrylic/25 per cent wool bulky weight yarn (135 metres (148 yds)/100g per ball): 9 (11, 13, 14, 15, 16) balls deep taupe #03020
• 5.5mm (size 9) needles or size needed to obtain gauge
• 8mm (size 11) double-pointed needles (2 for I-cord trim)
• Stitch marker

Gauge

21 sts and 24 rows = 10cm/4 inches in pat with smaller needles To save time, take time to check gauge.

Pattern Stitch
Tweed Mock Rib

(even number of sts)
Row 1 (RS): K1, *sl 1 purlwise, k1, yo, pass sl st over k1 and yo; rep from * to last st, k1.
Row 2: Purl across.
Rep Rows 1 and 2 for pat.

Back

With smaller needles, cast on 100 (110, 122, 132, 142, 154) sts and work in Tweed Mock Rib pat until back measures 39 (40.5, 40.5, 42, 43, 43)cm or 15½ (16, 16, 16½, 17, 17) inches from beg, ending with a WS row.

Shape armholes

Bind off 10 sts at beg of next 2 rows. (80, 90, 102, 112, 122, 134 sts)

Work in established pat until back measures 61 (63.5, 64.5, 66, 68.5, 70)cm or 24 (25, 25½, 26, 27, 27½) inches from beg, ending with a WS row.

Shape shoulders

Work across 24 (26, 27, 30, 32, 38) sts, join 2nd ball of yarn and bind off centre 32 (38, 48, 52, 58, 58) sts; complete row. Working both sides at once with separate balls of yarn,

work 2 more rows, then bind off rem sts in pat.

Right Front

With smaller needles, cast on 50 (56, 60, 66, 72, 76) sts and work in Tweed Mock Rib pat until front measures 35.5cm (14 inches) from beg, ending with a WS row.

Beg lapel

Work 1 st in purl (Row 2 of pat), place marker; work to end of row in established pat (Row 1 of pat).
Next row: Work Row 2 of pat to marker; then work 1 st in knit (Row 1 of pat).

Continue to work in this manner, working body in established pat and reversing pat on lapel sts. Move marker over 1 st every 3rd row, adding 1 new st to lapel, working sts into pat until there are 16 (20, 23, 26, 30, 28) lapel sts. *At the same time,* when front measures 39 (40.5, 40.5, 42, 43, 43)cm or 15½ (16, 16, 16½, 17, 17) inches, ending with a RS row, bind off 10 sts at beg of next row for armhole. (40, 46, 50, 56, 62, 66 sts)

Continue to work even in pat until armhole measures 18 (19,

20.5, 20.5, 21.5, 23)cm or 7 (7½, 8, 8, 8½, 9) inches above bind off, ending with a WS row. Bind off 16 (20, 23, 26, 30, 28) lapel sts. (24, 26, 27, 30, 32, 38 sts)

Work even on rem sts for another 5cm (2 inches). Bind off all sts.

Left Front
With smaller needles, cast on 50 (56, 60, 66, 72, 76) sts and work as for right front until front measures 35.5cm (14 inches) from beg, ending with a WS row.

Beg lapel
Work in established pat to last st (Row 1 of pat), place marker; purl 1 st (Row 2 of pat).
Next row: K1 (Row 1 of pat), purl across row (Row 2 of pat).

Continue to work in this manner, working body in established pat and reversing pat on lapel sts. Move marker over 1 st every 3rd row, adding 1 new st to lapel, working sts into pat until there are 16 (20, 23, 26, 30, 28) lapel sts. *At the same time*, when front measures 39 (40.5, 40.5, 42, 43, 43)cm or 15½ (16, 16, 16½, 17, 17) inches, ending with a WS

row, bind off 10 sts at beg of next row for armhole. (40, 46, 50, 56, 62, 66 sts)

Continue to work even in pat until armhole measures 18 (19, 20.5, 20.5, 21.5, 23)cm or 7 (7½, 8, 8, 8½, 9) inches above bind off, ending with a RS row. Bind off 16 (20, 23, 26, 30, 28) lapel sts. (24, 26, 27, 30, 32, 38 sts)

Work even on rem sts for another 5cm (2 inches). Bind off all sts.

Sleeves
With smaller needles, cast on 42 (48, 52, 54, 58, 60) sts and work in pat, inc 1 st at each end [every 3 (4, 4, 4, 4, 4) rows] 20 (20, 20, 26, 25, 28) times, then [every 6 (4, 4, 0, 4, 0) rows] 7 (6, 7, 0, 2, 0) times. (96, 100, 106, 106, 112, 116 sts)

Work even until piece measures 48.5 (51, 53.5, 53.5, 53.5, 56)cm or 19 (20, 21, 21, 21, 22) inches or desired length. Bind off all sts.

Assembly
Seam shoulders together neatly.

Collar
With smaller needles, WS of back and RS of left front lapel

facing, beg 4cm (1½ inches) in from edge of lapel, pick up and knit 68 (74, 82, 88, 92, 96) sts evenly, ending 4cm (1½ inches) from edge of right front lapel.

Turn and work in pat, beg with Row 2 (WS). Work even until collar measures 5cm (2 inches) or desired width. Bind off all sts.

Finishing
Sew sleeves into armholes; sew sleeve and side seams.

I-Cord Trim
Beg at lower right front side seam with larger dpn and RS facing, cast on 3 sts. *Slide sts to other end of needle, k2, work ssk with last I-cord st and 1 st picked up from jacket; rep from * around, working last I-cord st tog with approximately every 'mock rib' or every other row of jacket. Work around entire jacket edge, adjusting rate as needed to keep cord from being too loose or too tight and puckering jacket. Weave end of I-cord to beg.

Note: *If desired, I-cord may be knitted separately and sewn on.*

Block as needed. Lapels may need to be tacked down after blocking.** ◆

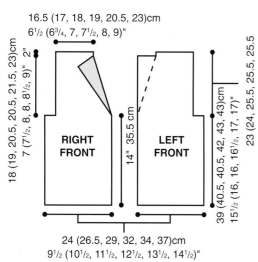

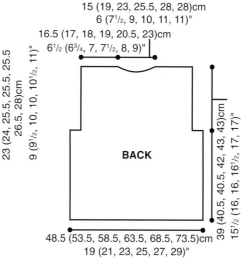

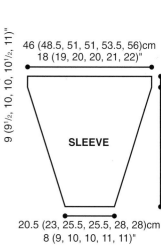

Easy Zoom Jacket

Reverse Stockinette stitch and naturally rolled edges add a trendy look to a short jacket.

DESIGN BY KENNITA TULLY

EASY

Size

Woman's small (medium, large, extra-large) instructions are given for smallest size, with larger sizes in parentheses. When only 1 number is given, it applies to all sizes.

Finished Measurements

Chest: 96.5 (106.5, 117, 127)cm or 38 (42, 46, 50) inches
Length: 46 (48.5, 51, 53.5)cm or 18 (19, 20, 21) inches

Materials

- Brown Sheep Prairie Silks 72 per cent wool/18 per cent mohair/10 per cent silk worsted weight yarn (80 metres (88 yds)/50g per hank): 10 (11, 12, 13) hanks green back #PS850
- 5mm (size 8) needles or size needed to obtain gauge
- 3 2.5-cm (1-inch) buttons
- Stitch markers

Gauge

16 sts and 24 rows = 10cm/4 inches in reverse St st
To save time, take time to check gauge.

Pattern Notes

All incs are worked 1 st from edge by making a backwards lp and placing on RH needle.

If desired, sleeves may be worked cuffed back.

Back

Cast on 78 (86, 94, 102) sts.

Work even in reverse St st until back measures 24 (25.5, 26.5, 28)cm or 9½ (10, 10½, 11) inches, ending with a WS row.

Shape armhole

Next 2 rows: Bind off 8 (9, 10, 12) sts, work to end of row. (62, 68, 74, 78 sts)

Work even until armhole measures 21.5 (23, 24, 25.5)cm or 8½ (9, 9½, 10) inches.

Bind off all sts.

Mark centre 28 (30, 32, 34) sts for back neck.

Left Front

Cast on 44 (48, 52, 56) sts.

Work even in reverse St st until front measures 24 (25.5, 26.5, 28)cm or 9½ (10, 10½, 11) inches, ending with a WS row.

Shape armhole

Next row (RS): Bind off 8 (9, 10, 12) sts, work to end of row. (36, 39, 42, 44 sts)

Work even until armhole measures same as for back.

Shape shoulder and back collar

Next row (RS): Bind off 17 (19, 21, 22) sts, work to end of row.

Work even on rem 19 (20, 21, 22) sts until collar measures 9 (9.5, 10, 11)cm or 3½ (3¾, 4, 4¼) inches.

Bind off.

Right Front

Work as for left front, except work armhole and shoulder bind-off rows on WS of work.

At the same time, make 3 buttonholes, having first one 7.5 (7.5, 10, 10)cm or 3½ (3½, 4, 4) inches from lower edge and spacing rem 9cm (3½ inches) apart.

Buttonhole row (RS): P3, bind off 3 sts, purl to end of row. On following row, cast on 3 sts over previously bound-off sts.

Sleeves

Cast on 36 (38, 40, 42) sts.

Work in reverse St st, inc 1 st each end [every 6th row] 6 (10, 14, 18) times, then [every 8th row] 10 (7, 4, 1) times. (68, 72, 76, 80 sts)

Mark each st of last row for underarm.

Work even for 5 (5.5, 6.5, 7.5)cm or 2 (2¼, 2½, 3) inches more. Bind off all sts.

Assembly

Sew shoulder seams.

Sew short ends of collar sections tog at centre back.

Sew long edge of collar to back neck.

Fold collar to outside and tack to back neck between shoulders.

Sew sleeves into armholes, matching markers to first bound-off st of underarm.

Sew sleeve and side seams.

Sew on buttons. ◆

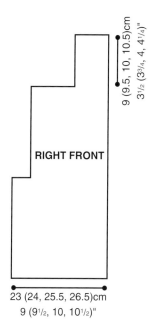

RIGHT FRONT

9 (9.5, 10, 10.5)cm
3½ (3¾, 4, 4¼)"

21.5 (23, 24, 25.5)cm
8½ (9, 9½, 10)"

24 (25.5, 26.5, 28)cm
9½ (10, 10½, 11)"

23 (24, 25.5, 26.5)cm
9 (9½, 10, 10½)"

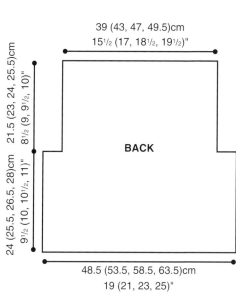

39 (43, 47, 49.5)cm
15½ (17, 18½, 19½)"

BACK

48.5 (53.5, 58.5, 63.5)cm
19 (21, 23, 25)"

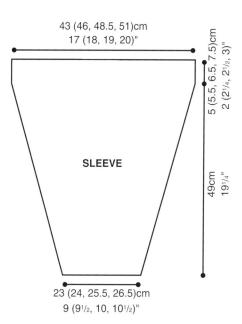

43 (46, 48.5, 51)cm
17 (18, 19, 20)"

5 (5.5, 6.5, 7.5)cm
2 (2¼, 2½, 3)"

SLEEVE

49cm
19¼"

23 (24, 25.5, 26.5)cm
9 (9½, 10, 10½)"

Make-In-a-Hurry Tabard

For quick results, or when time is at a premium, knit up a new look vest with bulky weight yarn.

DESIGN BY SVETLANA AVRAKH FOR BERNAT

EASY

Size
Woman's extra small/medium (large/2X-large, 3X/5X-large) instructions are given for smallest size, with larger sizes in parentheses. When only 1 number is given, it applies to all sizes.

Finished Size
Each panel measures approximately 24 (31.5, 39)cm or 9½ (12½, 15½) x 73.5 (79, 91.5)cm or 29 (31, 36) inches

Materials
- Bernat Black Lites 100 per cent acrylic bulky weight yarn (55 metres (60 yds)/100g per ball): 11 (12, 13) balls saffron silk #82030
- 6.5mm (size 10½) circular needle
- 8mm (size 11) needles or size needed to obtain gauge

Gauge
10½ sts and 14 rows = 10cm/4 inches in St st with larger needles

To save time, take time to check gauge.

Right Side
With larger needles, cast on 25 (33, 41) sts.
Row 1 (RS): K1, *yo, k2tog; rep from * to last 2 sts, end k2.
Row 2: K2, purl across.
Row 3: *Ssk, yo; rep from * to last 3 sts, end k3.
Row 4: Rep Row 2.
Rep Rows 1–4 until piece measures 73.5 (79, 91.5)cm or 29 (31, 36) inches from beg, ending with a WS row. Bind off all sts.

Left Side
With larger needles, cast on 25 (33, 41) sts.
Row 1 (RS): K3, *yo, k2tog; rep from * across.
Row 2: Purl to last 2 sts, k2.
Row 3: K2, *ssk, yo; rep from * to last st, k1.
Row 4: Rep Row 2.
Rep Rows 1–4 until piece measures 73.5 (79, 91.5)cm or 29 (31, 36) inches from beg, ending with a WS row. Bind off all sts.

Assembly
Sew left and right sides tog, having 2 garter sts at outer edges and leaving 48cm (19 inches) open in middle of seam for neck.

With circular needle, pick up and knit 42 (50, 62) sts along cast-on edges of right and left sides and 42 (50, 62) sts along bound-off edges of right and left sides. Join to work in rnds. (84, 100, 124 sts)
Rnd 1: *K2, p2; rep from * around.
Rep Rnd 1 until ribbing measures 12.5cm (5 inches).
Bind off in rib. ◆

Double-Increase Shawl

Three colours of yarn and a funky double increase create this striking, versatile shawl.

DESIGN BY BETH WHITESIDE

EASY

Finished Size
Approximately 140 x 54.5cm (55 x 21½ inches)

Materials
- Reynolds/JCA Soft Sea Wool 100 per cent wool DK weight wool yarn (148 metres (162 yds)/50g per skein): 1 skein each magenta #941 (A), purple #320 (B), green #650 (C)
- 6.5mm (size 10½) 61-cm (24-inch) circular needle or size needed to obtain gauge
- Stitch markers

Gauge
15 sts and 26½ rows = 10cm/4 inches in Garter Dot St pat
To save time, take time to check gauge.

Special Abbreviation
KOK: Inc 2 sts by working [k1, yo, k1] in next st.

Pattern Stitch
Garter Dot St
Row 1 (RS): With MC, k1, yo, k1, knit to centre st, KOK, knit to last 2 sts, end k1, yo, k1.

Row 2: K2, [k1, p1] to centre 3 sts, k3, [p1, k1] to last 2 sts, end k2.

Rows 3–10: [Rep Rows 1 and 2] 4 times.

Row 11: K1, yo, k1, knit to marker, M1L, knit to centre st, KOK, knit to marker, M1R, knit to last 2 sts, end k1, yo, k1.

Row 12: Knit across.

Row 13: K1, yo, k1, knit to centre st, KOK, knit to last 2 sts, end k1, yo, k1.

Row 14: Knit across.

Rows 15 and 16: With CC, rep Rows 13 and 14.

Row 17: Rep Row 13

Row 18: Knit across.

Rows 19 and 20: With CC, rep Rows 11 and 12.
Rep Rows 1–20 for pat.

Pattern Notes
This basic shawl is created by adding 1 st on each end and 2 sts in the middle of every other row. In garter st this method would create the perfect shape for draping over your shoulders; the taller row gauge of Dot St requires some additional inc to create the same shape.

A total of 44 sts is added in the 20-row rep of Garter Dot St; 1 st at each end plus 2 side-by-side in the centre of every right side row, and 1 additional st in the middle of each shawl half on Rows 11 and 19.

Circular needles are used to accommodate large number of sts. Do not join; work back and forth in rows.

Shawl
With A, make a sl knot on 1 needle. Work a KOK inc (3 sts)
Knit 1 row.

Row 1 (RS): K1, yo, KOK, yo, k1. (7 sts)

Rows 2 and 4: Knit across.

Row 3: K1, yo, k2, KOK, k2, yo, k1. (11 sts)

Row 5: K1, yo, k2, place marker, k2, KOK, k2, place marker, k2, yo, k1. (15 sts)

Row 6: Knit across.

Beg pat, alternating colours as follows:

Rows 1–20: Work Rows 1–20 of Garter Dot St pat; A is MC, B is CC. (15 + 44 sts added = 59 sts)

Rows 21–40: Rep Rows 1–20; B is MC, C is CC. (59 + 44 sts added = 103 sts)

Rows 41–60: Rep Rows 1–20; C is MC, A is CC. (103 + 44 sts added = 147 sts)

Rows 61–100: Rep Rows 1–40.

Rows 101–118: Rep Rows 1–18.

Rows 119 and 120: With A, rep Rows 1 and 2.

Rows 121 and 122: With B, rep Rows 1 and 2.

Eyelet Edging

With A, k1 [yo, k2tog] to 3 centre sts, k3, [k2tog, yo] to last st, end k1. Bind off all sts knitwise.

Steam-block lightly. ◆

Magical Möbius

Dropped stitches make a light and airy fabric. A twist before seaming creates the Möbius strip. Magic!

DESIGN BY KRISTIN OMDAHL

BEGINNER

Finished Size
56 x 112cm (22 x 44 inches) (before seaming)

Materials

- Plymouth Yesterday 80 per cent mohair/15 per cent wool/5 per cent nylon bulky weight yarn (101 metres (110 yds)/50g per ball): 3 balls brown multi #1703 (A)
- Plymouth Eros 100 per cent nylon medium weight yarn (151 metres (165 yds)/50g per ball): 2 balls brown multi #7132 (B)
- 6.5mm (size 10.5) straight needles or size needed to obtain gauge
- Tapestry needle

Gauge
12 sts and 12 rows = 10cm/4 inches garter st with A and B held tog
To save time, take time to check gauge.

Pattern Note
Möbius is worked holding 1 strand A and B held tog throughout.

Möbius
With A and B held tog, cast on 47 sts.

Knit 140 rows. (70 garter ridges)

[*Bind off 5 sts, cut yarn and pull through last st to fasten off*, reattach yarn and k2] 6 times, work from * to *. Slide rem 12 sts off needles and gently drop sts down to cast-on edge.

Finishing
Weave in all ends.

Gently wash the scarf in lukewarm water and dry flat pinned at finished measurements.

With the rectangle facing you, twist 1 side 180 degrees and pin both short edges tog, matching corners A and D, and B and C (see diagram).

Sew the garter sections tog carefully and invisibly. ◆

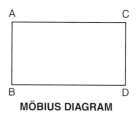

MÖBIUS DIAGRAM

Naturally Biased Scarf

This easy scarf is shaped to fit nicely around your shoulders.

DESIGN BY BETH WHITESIDE

EASY

Finished Size
Approximately 26.5cm (10½ inches) wide

Materials
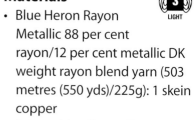
3 LIGHT

- Blue Heron Rayon Metallic 88 per cent rayon/12 per cent metallic DK weight rayon blend yarn (503 metres (550 yds)/225g): 1 skein copper
- 5.5mm (size 9) needles or size needed to obtain gauge

Gauge
17 sts = 10cm/4 inches in Unbiased Yo pat
Exact gauge is not critical to this project.

Pattern Stitches
A. Bias Pat 1 (right slant)
Row 1 (RS): K2, *yo, k2tog; rep from * to last 2 sts, end k2.
Row 2: K2, purl to last 2 sts, k2.
Rep Rows 1 and 2 for pat.

B. Bias Pat 2 (left slant)
Row 1 (RS): K2, *ssk, yo; rep from * to last 2 sts, end k2.
Row 2: K2, purl to last 2 sts, k2.
Rep Rows 1 and 2 for pat.

C. Unbiased Yo Pat (no slant)
Row 1 (RS): K2, *ssk, yo; rep from * to last 2 sts, end k2.
Rows 2 and 4: K2, purl to last 2 sts, k2.
Row 3: K2, *yo, k2tog; rep from * to last 2 sts, k2.
Rep Rows 1–4 for pat.

Pattern Notes
The Naturally Biased Scarf has 3 sections. The centre section combines yarn overs with right and left slanting dec to produce a lacy vertical pat. The 2 end sections illustrate the biased, or diagonal, fabric that results when dec with the same slant are stacked on top of each other row after row.

Note that the yo is worked before the dec in Bias Pat 1 and after the dec in Bias Pat 2.

Use Cable Cast On (see page 8) throughout.

Scarf
Picot cast on 46 sts: Using cable cast on, cast on 4 sts, bind off 2 sts and replace st on LH needle, [cast on 5 sts, bind off 2 sts and replace st on LH needle] 14 times, end cast on 2 sts.

Purl 3 rows.

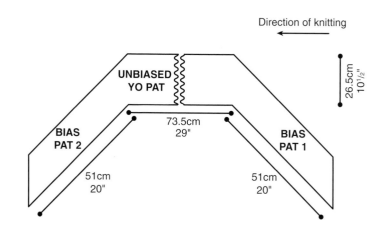

Direction of knitting

UNBIASED YO PAT

BIAS PAT 2

BIAS PAT 1

73.5cm 29"

51cm 20"

51cm 20"

26.5cm 10½"

Work in Bias Pat 1 for 96 rows or until work measures 51cm (20 inches) along slanting edge.

Change to Unbiased Yo Pat, working until centre section measures 73.5cm (29 inches) (approximately 132 rows).

Work in Bias Pat 2 for 96 rows or until this section measures 51cm (20 inches) along slanting edge.

Purl 3 rows.

Picot bind off: Bind off 1 st, replace st on LH needle, [cast on 2 sts, bind off 5 sts, replace st on LH needle] 14 times, cast on 2 sts, bind off 4 sts. Fasten off. ◆

Self-Fringed Scarf

This scarf is a beginner knit that gets its pizzazz from a fringe all the way down the length. The easy fringe is created by dropping the last few stitches after the simple garter scarf is all knitted!

DESIGN BY JULIE GADDY

BEGINNER

Finished Size
Approximately 28 x 140cm (11 x 55 inches) (excluding fringe)

Materials
- Caron International Simply Soft Shadows 100 per cent acrylic worsted weight yarn (137 metres (150 yds)/85g per skein): 4 skeins autumn red #0004
- 5mm (size 8) needles or size needed to obtain gauge

Gauge
18 sts = 10cm/4 inches in garter st

Exact gauge is not critical to this project.

Pattern Notes
Always add new skein at the edge.

The 'tail' will vanish in the fringe, and you won't have any ends to hide in the scarf fabric.

Scarf
Cast on 60 sts. Knit even in garter st until approximately 275cm (3 yds) of yarn rem, or until scarf is desired length.

K5, bind off knitwise until 5 sts rem, k5. Remove needle from work.

Fringe
Unravel 5 live (not bound-off) sts on each edge. Knot each lp of fringe near base to form a stable edge. For ease in working, only unravel a few rows at a time.

Block scarf to finished measurements by washing and placing flat to dry. Do not steam.

Trim fringe even, if desired. Alternatively, you may leave lps along edges for another look! ✦

Weave a Little Colour

Add contrast colour stripes after you are done knitting this anyone-can-knit set.

DESIGN BY ANNA TAPP

Scarf

EASY

Finished Size
Approximately 137 x 14cm
(54 x 5½ inches)

Materials
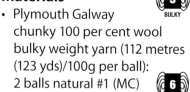
- Plymouth Galway chunky 100 per cent wool bulky weight yarn (112 metres (123 yds)/100g per ball): 2 balls natural #1 (MC)
- Plymouth Hand Paint 100 per cent wool super bulky weight yarn (60 metres (66 yds)/100g per skein): 1 skein #160 (CC)
- 9mm (size 13) needles or size needed to obtain gauge
- Stitch holder
- Yarn needle

Gauge
12 sts and 13 rows = 10cm/4 inches in St st with MC
To save time, take time to check gauge.

Pattern Stitch
K3, P3 Rib (multiple of 6 sts)
Row 1: *K3, p3; rep from * across. Rep Row 1 for pat.

Pattern Note
Scarf is reversible.

Beg Fringe
[With MC, cast on 3 sts; work 15 rows in St st; cut yarn, place sts on holder or spare needle] 8 times. (24 sts and 8 fringes on holder)

Place fringes on left needle, beg by placing first fringe with WS facing, and alternating between RS and WS facing.

Scarf
Work in k3, p3 rib across 24 sts until scarf measures approximately 112cm (44 inches), excluding fringe.

Ending Fringe
*Work first 3 sts in St st for 14 rows. Bind off 3 sts. Rep from * until all sts are worked, alternating knit and purl sides as for beg fringe.

Block scarf to approximately 14-cm (5½-inch) width.

Stripes
Referring to photo, with MC and yarn needle, being careful not to pull too snug, weave 1 strand of MC back and forth across every other row of rib, going under k3 rib and over p3, so strand shows on purl side of rib.

Cut 8 (152-cm/60-inch) lengths of CC. Weave CC under 2 strands of MC, then over 2 strands along length of scarf. Trim CC even with fringes.

Hat

INTERMEDIATE

Size
Woman's medium (large) instructions are given for medium, with larger size in parentheses. When only 1 number is given, it applies to both sizes.

Finished Measurement
To fit 51-cm (56-cm) or 20-inch (22-inch) head

Materials

- Plymouth Galway chunky 100 per cent wool bulky weight yarn (100g/123 yds per ball): 1 ball natural #1 (MC)
- Plymouth Hand Paint 100 per cent wool super bulky weight yarn (100g/66 yds per skein): 1 skein #160 (CC)
- 9mm (size 13) set of double-pointed needles or size needed to obtain gauge
- Yarn needle

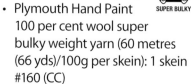
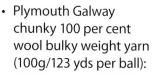

Gauge

12 sts and 13 rows = 10cm/4 inches in St st with MC
To save time, take time to check gauge.

Special Abbreviation

M1 (Make 1): Inc 1 st by lifting strand between st just worked and next st, place on LH needle, k1-tbl.

Pattern Stitch

(multiple of 4 sts)
Rnd 1 (RS): *Yo, ssk, k2; rep from * around.
Rnd 2: Knit.
Rnd 3: *K2, k2tog, yo; rep from * around.
Rnd 4: Knit.
Rep Rnds 1–4 for pat.

Hat

With CC, cast on 36 (42) sts, placing 12 (14) sts on each needle. Mark beg of rnd and join without twisting.
Rnds 1–5 (7): *K2, p1; rep from * around.
Rnd 6 (8): Change to MC, *M1, k3; rep from * around. (48, 56 sts)
Beg pat and work even until hat measures 28 (30.5)cm or 11 (12) inches or desired length. Bind off in pat.

Stripes

Referring to photo, weave CC up and down through spaces. Rep for all spaces in hat.
With yarn needle and MC, work a running st through pat around top of hat. Pull tight and fasten securely.

Tassel

Cut a 19-sq-cm (3-inch-square) piece of stiff cardboard. Wind CC around cardboard 25 times. Cut an 46cm (18-inch) length of CC and insert it under all of strands at top of cardboard. Pull tightly and tie securely. Cut loops at opposite end of cardboard. Cut a 30.5-cm (12-inch) length of MC and wrap it tightly around tassel repeatedly, approximately 1.5cm (½ inch) below top. Tie securely. Trim tassel ends and fasten tassel securely to gathered top of hat.

Mittens

INTERMEDIATE

Size

Woman's medium (large) instructions are given for medium, with large in parentheses. When only 1 number is given, it applies to both sizes.

Finished Size

Fits up to 18-cm (23-cm) or 7-inch (9-inch) hand

Materials

- Plymouth Galway chunky 100 per cent wool bulky weight yarn (112 metres (123 yds)/100g per ball): 1 ball natural #1 (MC)
- Plymouth Hand Paint 100 per cent wool super bulky weight yarn (55 metres (60 yds)/100g per skein): 1 skein #160 (CC)
- 6mm (size 10) double-pointed needles or size needed to obtain gauge
- Stitch markers
- Stitch holders
- Yarn needle

Gauge

12 sts and 17 rows = 10cm/4 inches in St st with MC
To save time, take time to check gauge.

Pattern Stitch

K2, P2 Rib (multiple of 4 sts)
Rnd 1: *K2, p2; rep from * around.
Rep Rnd 1 for pat.

Mitten
Make 2 alike

Cuff

With CC, cast on 32 (38) sts. Place 12 (14) sts on first needle and 10 (12) sts each on next 2 needles. Mark beg of rnd and join without twisting.
Rnds 1–4: *K2, p2; rep from * around.
Change to MC and continue in K2, P2 Rib until mitten measures 10 (11.5)cm or 4 (4½) inches from beg.

Thumb opening

Place first 4 sts on holder, cast on 4 sts, continue in K2, P2 Rib around.

Mitten top

Continue in K2, P2 Rib until mitten measures 23 (25.5)cm or 9 (10) inches from beg.
Dec rnd: [K2tog, p2tog] around. Cut yarn.

CONTINUED ON PAGE 153

Autumn's Glory

The rich shades of autumn's splendid foliage are captured in a warm, diagonal-striped scarf and matching snug beret.

DESIGN BY DIANE ELLIOTT

EASY

Size
One size fits most

Finished Measurements
Scarf: Approximately 12.5 x 152cm (5 x 60 inches)
Hat circumference: 48.5cm (19 inches)

Materials
- Brown Sheep Handpaint Originals 70 per cent mohair/30 per cent wool worsted weight yarn (80 metres (88 yds)/50g per hank): 2 hanks each New England Fall #HP80 (MC) and chestnut #HP35 (CC)
- 4mm (size 6) needles
- 6.5mm (size 10½) needles or size needed to obtain gauge
- Stitch markers

4 MEDIUM

Gauge
13 sts and 20 rows = 10cm/4 inches in St st with larger needles
To save time, take time to check gauge.

Pattern Stitch
1/1 Ribbing
Row 1 (RS): K1, *p1, k1; rep from * across.
Row 2: P1, *k1, p1; rep from * across.
Rep Rows 1 and 2 for pat.

Pattern Notes
Work pat inc by knitting in top of st in row below.

Carry yarn not in use up side of work; do not cut yarn after colour change.

Scarf
With MC and larger needles, cast on 23 sts.
Foundation row (WS): K1, *p1, k1; rep from * across.
Rows 1, 3 and 5: With MC, k1, inc in next st, knit to last 3 sts, k2tog, k1.
Rows 2, 4 and 6: With MC, k1 *p1, k1; rep from * across.
Rows 7 and 9: With CC, rep Row 1.
Rows 8 and 10: With CC, rep Row 2.

Rep Rows 1–10 until scarf measures approximately 152cm (60 inches), ending with Row 6 of pat.

Next row: K1, *p1, k1; rep from * across.

    Bind off.

Hat

With CC and smaller needles, cast on 100 sts.

    Work even in 1/1 Ribbing for 3cm (1¼ inches), inc 9 sts evenly on last WS row. (109 sts)

Rows 1, 3 and 5 (RS): With MC, k1, inc in next st, k50, k2tog, pm, k1, inc in next, k50, k2tog, k1.

Rows 2, 4 and 6: With MC, k1 *p1, k1; rep from * across.

Rows 7 and 9: With CC, rep Row 1.

Rows 8 and 10: With CC, rep Row 2.

    [Work Rows 1–10] twice, rep Rows 1–4.

Shape top

Row 1: With MC, *k1, inc in next st, [k8, k2tog] 5 times, k2tog; rep from * once, k1. (99 sts)

Row 2: With MC, k1 *p1, k1; rep from * across.

Row 3: With CC, *k1, inc in next st, [k7, k2tog] 5 times, k2tog; rep from * once, k1. (89 sts)

Rows 4 and 6: With CC, rep Row 2.

Row 5: *K1, inc in next st [k6, k2tog] 5 times, k2tog; rep from * once, k1. (79 sts)

Row 7: *K2tog, k1; rep from * to last 4 sts, [k2tog] twice. (52 sts)

Row 8: Purl.

Row 9: K2tog across. (26 sts)

Row 10: P2tog across. (13 sts)

Finishing

Cut yarn, leaving a 61-cm (24-inch) end. Draw yarn through rem sts twice and pull tightly to close opening.

    Sew seam. ◆

Roll the Dice Tote Bag

Feeling lucky? Decide when to change colours by rolling the dice!

DESIGN BY CINDY ADAMS

EASY

Finished Size

Approximately 38 x 43cm (15 x 17 inches), depending on felting

Materials

4 MEDIUM

- Patons Classic Merino 100 per cent merino worsted weight wool yarn (204 metres (223 yds)/100g per ball): 1 ball each Aran #00202, maize #00203, deep olive #00205, old rose #00209, petal pink #00210, leaf green #00240
- 8mm (size 11) needles or size needed to obtain gauge

Gauge

10 sts and 20 rows (10 ridges) = 10cm/4 inches in garter st Exact gauge is not critical; make sure your stitches are loose and airy. Tight knitting will not felt as quickly.

Pattern Notes

Dice, money and cheating? Pick 6 colours of yarn and assign a number one through six to each colour. Roll the die to decide which colour to use. Roll the die again to decide how many ridges to knit. Roll it one more time to decide at what point in the row to change colours. One is near the beginning and six is near the end etc.

Paper money is used to determine the length of the fringe. Use a note to measure the length of fringe.

Cheating (don't try this at the tables!) is allowed just in case you don't like the roll of the dice.

Bag

Using first colour, cast on 75 sts.
Row 1 (WS): Sl 1, knit across.
Row 2: Sl 1, inc 1, knit to last 3 sts, end k2tog, k1.

Rep Rows 1 and 2, changing colours according to dice (or cheat if desired).

Change colours on RS, leaving knots. Solid colour ridges are counted at beg of row for colour change. Rep Rows 1 and 2 until piece measures approximately 117–127cm (46–50 inches) along a side edge.

Assembly

Slip cast-on sts on an extra needle, bind off beg and end, using 3-Needle Bind Off (see page 9), or bind off and sl st to cast-on row. This forms a diagonal seam.

With RS tog, fold purse in half. Seam 1 edge for bottom, leave other edge open.

After bag is sewn tog, cut about 24–30 pieces of fringe about 15cm (6 inch). Fold in half and attach 1 piece (or 2) of fringe beside a knot of same colour. After felting, trim all fringe to about 2.5cm (1 inch).

Handles
Make 2

With one colour, cast on 5 sts. Knit 8 rows. Cut yarn. Cast on another 5 sts and knit 8 rows.

On next row, knit across all 10 sts. Knit 40 rows (20 ridges). Working on first 5 sts only, knit 8 rows, bind off. Attach yarn and knit 8 rows on rem 5 sts, bind off.

Fold handle in half lengthwise, and sew tog on the 10-st rows, leaving 5-st tabs open. Referring to photo, position handle on bag, placing 1 tab on inside and 1 on outside. Sew securely with matching yarn.

Felting

See instructions on page 72. ◆

Felted Bags to Give

You choose the size for these quick-to-make bags.

DESIGN BY ELLEN EDWARDS DRECHSLER

EASY

Compact & Cute Bag

Finished Size

Approximately 24 x 15cm (9½ x 6 inches) (after felting)

Materials

- Lion Brand Landscapes 50 per cent wool/50 per cent acrylic super bulky wool-blend yarn (50 metres (55 yds)/50g per ball): 3 balls pastel meadows #272
- 9mm (size 13) needles
- Stitch markers
- Stitch holders
- Snap set

Gauge

10 sts = 10cm/4 inches in garter st (before felting)
Exact gauge is not critical to this project.

Pattern Notes

Bag should measure approximately 35.5 x 23cm (14 x 9 inches) before felting; 24 x 15cm (9½ x 6 inches) after felting. Sample bag was worked with yarn given; results may vary with a different yarn.

Bag is made in garter stitch and is worked from side to side. Looking at the photo, the edge on the right side of the photo is the cast-on edge. Work from that side increasing at each end every other row, then work the handle. Go back and work the bag body (straight section under the handle). The handle stitches are put back on the needle with the body stitches. Begin decreasing every other row to the original number of stitches. Bind off. This resembles a large mug with the handle on the right-hand side.

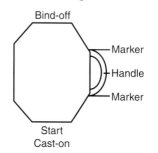

Bind-off

Marker

Handle

Marker

Start
Cast-on

Compact & Cute Bag Make 2

Cast on 10 sts. Beg on next row, inc 1 st at beg and end every other row until there are 26 sts. Place a marker on edge of knitting. Knit 3 rows even. On 3rd row, on edge with marker, attach a new ball of yarn and knit on first 4 sts until you have completed 14 garter ridges (28 rows), ending at outside edge away from bag. Leave sts on a holder.

With a separate ball of yarn, knit even on bag body sts until opening measures 12.5cm (5 inches), ending at edge with marker. Sl strap sts onto needle and knit 3 rows even on all sts. Place a marker at strap edge.

Beg on next row, dec 2 sts every other row by k2tog at beg of row and ssk at end of row until 10 sts rem. Bind off.

Assembly

Sew pieces tog, beg and ending at markers.

Felt bag, following directions on page 72. Let air dry. Sew a snap set inside bag under handles.

Big & Roomy Bag

Finished Size

Approximately 42 x 31.5cm (16½ x 12½ inches) (after felting)

Materials

- Lion Brand Landscapes 50 per cent wool/50 per cent acrylic super bulky wool-blend yarn (50g/55 yds per ball): 7 balls rose garden #271
- 9mm (size 13) needles
- Stitch markers
- Stitch holders
- Button

Gauge

10 sts = 10cm/4 inches in garter
st (before felting)
Exact gauge is not critical to this
project.

Pattern Notes

Bag should measure
approximately 68.5 x 51cm (27
x 20 inches) before felting; 42 x
31.5cm (16½ x 12½ inches) after
felting. Sample bag was worked
with yarn given; results may vary
with a different yarn.

Big & Roomy Bag
Make 2

Cast on 10 sts. Beg on next row,
inc 1 st at beg and end every
other row until there are 52

sts. Place a marker on edge of
knitting. Knit 3 rows even.

On 3rd row, on edge with
marker, attach a new ball of
yarn and knit on first 6 sts until
you have completed 20 garter
ridges (40 rows), ending at
outside edge away from bag.
Leave sts on a holder.

With a separate ball of yarn,
knit even on bag body sts until
opening measures 20.5cm
(8 inches), ending at edge with
marker. Sl strap sts onto needle
and knit 3 rows even on all sts.
Place a marker at strap edge.

Beg on next row, dec 2 sts
every other row by k2tog at beg
of row and ssk at end of row until
10 sts rem. Bind off.

Assembly

Sew pieces tog, beg and ending
at markers.

Button Tab

With RS facing, pick up and knit
8 sts under centre of handle on
1 side. Work in garter st for 8
ridges (16 rows), ending with a
WS row.
Buttonhole: K3, bind off 2 sts,
knit to end.
Next row: K3, cast on 2 sts, k3.

Knit 2 more ridges (4 rows)
even, then bind off all sts.

Felt bag according to
instructions on page 72. Let
air dry. Sew a button on bag
opposite buttonhole on tab. ◆

You've Got the Buttons Tote

Add an array of stacked black and white buttons or ad lib with your own button collection.

DESIGN BY ELLEN EDWARDS DRECHSLER

EASY

Finished Size
Approximately 79 x 25.5cm (31 x 10 inches) (after felting)

Materials
- Plymouth Galway 100 per cent wool worsted weight yarn (192 metres (210 yds)/100g per ball): 4 balls turquoise #139
- 9mm (size 13) circular and double-pointed needles or size needed to obtain gauge
- Stitch markers
- Buttons, as desired
- Black embroidery floss
- Large-eye sewing needle

Gauge
Approximately 12 sts = 10cm/4 inches in garter st with 2 strands held tog (before felting)
Exact gauge is not critical to this project.

Pattern Note
Project is worked with 2 strands of yarn held tog throughout.

Bottom
With 2 strands of yarn held tog, cast on 20 sts. Knit for 60 rows (30 ridges).

Sides
Place marker, pick up and knit 30 sts across long edge, place marker, pick up and knit 20 sts across short edge, place marker, pick up and knit 30 sts across rem long edge. (100 sts)

Join and knit in rnds until tote measures 40.5cm (16 inches) from beg.

Top
Knit 1 rnd, purl 1 rnd (garter st in rnds) until top measures approximately 5cm (2 inches). Bind off all sts.

I-Cord Handle
With 2 dpn and 2 strands of yarn, cast on 6 sts, *slide sts to other end of needle, pull yarn across back, k6, rep from * until cord measures approximately 86.5cm (34 inches). Fasten off.

Sew ends of cord to centre of sides of tote.

Felting
See felting instructions. Shape by placing a box inside a plastic bag into tote.

Finishing
Referring to photo, stack 3 or 4 buttons in alternating colours and use embroidery floss to sew to front of tote. ◆

Felting Instructions
Place bag in a pillowcase or mesh laundry bag. Set the washer to hot wash, cold rinse and lowest water level. Add a small amount of dish soap or laundry detergent. Add a pair of jeans to help in the agitation process. Check on the piece every 5 minutes. Felting could take 20–25 minutes or so. Keep setting back the timer to make the wash cycle longer. When desired felting is achieved, rinse and spin lightly. Excessive spinning can set in creases. Excess water can also be removed by rolling piece in a towel. Remove piece and stuff or stretch to desired shape. Let dry (may take up to 2 days).

Curlicue Beaded Necklace

If you haven't tried bead knitting, here's a super first project!

DESIGN BY CIA ABBOTT BULLEMER

EASY

Materials

SUPER FINE

- Plymouth Sockotta 45 per cent cotton/40 per cent superwash wool/15 per cent nylon sock yarn (379 metres (414 yds)/100g per ball): 1 ball multi #18
- 3.5mm (size 4) needles
- 172 size 6 beads
- Beading needle
- Hook and eye jewellery closure
- Tapestry needle
- Sewing needle and matching thread

Gauge

Approximately 13 sts = 5cm/2 inches

Exact gauge is not critical to this project.

Special Abbreviation

Dbl inc (double increase): Inc 2 sts by k1 in front lp, do not sl st off LH needle, sl bead, k1 into back lp, k1 into front lp again, sl st off LH needle in next st.

Pattern Notes

If you prefer a tighter twist, use a needle 1 size smaller.

Necklace is made in 2 strands. Before casting on, thread 172 beads on yarn.

Strand 1

Cast on 150 sts.

Row 1: Knit across.
Row 2: K38, dbl inc in each of next 74 sts, k38.

Bind off all sts. Cut yarn, leaving rem beads on yarn for 2nd strand.

Strand 2

Cast on 190 sts.

Row 1: Knit across.
Row 2: K46, dbl inc in each of next 98 sts, k46.

Bind off all sts.

Assembly

With tapestry needle and yarn ends, sew 2 strands tog at ends. Sew hook and eye closure to ends of strands. ◆

Star Pin

Create these clever stars to embellish everything from your lapel to your holiday tree.

DESIGN BY BETH CAMERA

EASY

Finished Measurement

Approximately 8-cm (3¼-inch) diameter

Materials

- Lion Brand Glitterspun 60 per cent acrylic/27 per cent Cupro/13 per cent polyester worsted weight metallic yarn (105 metres (115 yds)/50g per ball): 1 ball silver #150 (A), 1 ball onyx #153 (B)
- Kreinik Ombre Metallic 8-ply thread (15m (17 yds) per spool): 1 spool misty scarlet #1400 (C)
- 4.5mm (size 7) needles or size needed to obtain gauge
- 9mm Glass beads: 3 pale pink, 3 dark rose
- 2 (4-cm/1½-inch) pin backs

Gauge

4.5 sts = 2.5cm/1 inch in St st
Exact gauge is not critical to this project.

Special Abbreviation

MP (Make Petal): K1, sl st back to LH needle, turn, pass next 5 sts, 1 at a time, over first st, turn, k1 in first st.

Flowers

Bottom layer: Make 2, 1A & 1B. Holding A or B and C tog, cast on 73 sts.

Rows 1, 3, 5 and 7: Purl across.
Row 2 (petal row): [K1, MP, k1] 9 times, k1. (28 sts)
Row 4: [K2tog] 14 times. (14 sts)
Row 6: K1, [yo, k2tog] 6 times, k1. (14 sts)
Row 8: [K2tog] 7 times. (7 sts)

Cut yarn, leaving a 20.5-cm (8-inch) tail.

Using tapestry needle, thread tail through loose sts before taking flower off needle. Pull tight, weave in ends and sew up side to make circle.

Top layer: Make 2, 1A and 1B. Holding A or B and C tog, cast on 41 sts.

Rows 1, 3 and 5: Purl across.
Row 2 (petal row): [K1, MP, k1] 5 times, k1. (16 sts)
Row 4: K1, [yo, k2tog] 7 times, k1. (16 sts)
Row 6: [K2tog] 8 times. (8 sts)

Cut yarn and finish same as large flower.

Assembly

Place small flower onto large flower and sew in place. Referring to photo, centre 3 pale pink beads on 1 flower and 3 dark rose beads on the other; sew on using C. Sew on pin back. ◆

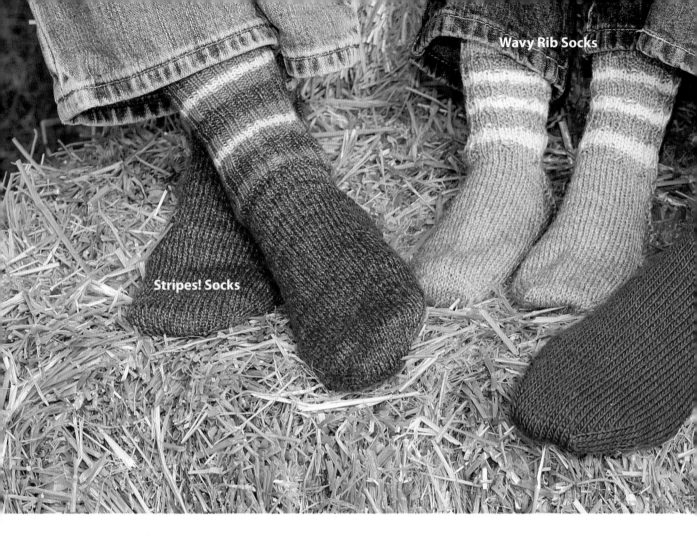

Wavy Rib Socks

Stripes! Socks

Family of Socks

Your whole family will have warm feet when you knit this variety of socks.

DESIGN BY EJ SLAYTON

Basket-Weave Socks

INTERMEDIATE

Man's small (medium, large) instructions are given for smallest size, with larger sizes in parentheses. When only 1 number is given, it applies to all sizes.

Finished Measurement

Circumference: Approximately 20 (23, 24.5)cm or 8¼ (9, 9¾) inches

Materials

SUPER FINE **1**

• Brown Sheep Wildfoote Luxury Sock Yarn 75 per cent washable wool/25 per cent nylon fingering weight yarn (197 metres (215 yds)/50g per ball):

Three-Colour Tweed Socks

Basket-Weave Socks

2 (2, 3) balls Zane Grey #SY36
- 2.25mm (size 1) double-pointed needles, or size needed to obtain gauge
- Stitch markers

Gauge
16 sts and 19 rnds = 5cm/2 inches in St st (blocked)
To save time, take time to check gauge.

Pattern Stitch
Basket Weave (multiple of 6 sts)
Rnds 1 and 2: Knit.
Rnds 3–6: *P4, k2; rep from * around.
Rnds 7 and 8: Knit.
Rnd 9: K3, *p4, k2; rep from * to last 3 sts, p3.
Rnds 10–12: P1, *k2, p4; rep

from *, end last rep p3.
Rep Rnds 1–12 for pat.

Sock
Cast on 64 (72, 76) sts.
Join without twisting, pm between first and last st.
Work in k2, p2 ribbing for 5cm (2 inches).
Beg pat, inc 2 (0, 2) sts evenly on first rnd. (66, 72, 78 sts)
Work even until top measures 20.5cm (8 inches) or desired length.
Knit 2 rnds, dec 2 (0, 2) sts evenly. (64, 72, 76 sts)

Heel
Sl next 32 (36, 38) sts to 1 needle for heel, divide rem 32 (36, 38) sts between 2 needles for instep.

Working in rows on heel sts only, knit across.
Row 1 (WS): Sl 1, purl across.
Row 2: *Sl 1, k1; rep from * across.
Rep Rows 1 and 2 until there are 16 (18, 19) lps on each side of heel flap, ending with Row 2.

Turn heel
Row 1 (WS): Sl 1, p17 (19, 20), p2tog, p1, turn.
Row 2: Sl 1, k5, k2tog, k1, turn.
Row 3: Sl 1, p6, p2tog, p1, turn.
Row 4: Sl 1, k7, k2tog, k1, turn.
Row 5: Sl 1, p8, p2tog, p1, turn.
Row 6: Sl 1, k9, k2tog, k1, turn.
Continue in this manner, working 1 more st before dec each time, until all sts have been worked. (18, 20, 22 sts)

Gusset

Needle 1: Working along right edge of heel flap, with needle containing heel sts, pick up and knit 16 (18, 19) sts (1 st in each lp);

Needle 2: Work instep sts onto 1 needle, *at the same time,* at each end, pick up either a st in the row below, or twist the running thread and knit it tog with the first and last st;

Needle 3: Pick up and knit 16 (18, 19) sts along left edge of heel flap, then knit 9 (10, 11) heel sts onto same needle. There will be 25 (28, 31) sts each on needles 1 and 3, and 32 (36, 38) sts on needle 2. (82, 92, 98 sts)

Rnd 1: Knit.

Rnd 2: Knit to last 3 sts of needle 1, k2tog, k1; knit across needle 2; on needle 3, k1, ssk, knit to end.

Rep Rnds 1 and 2 until needle 1 and needle 3 each contains 16 (18, 19) sts. (64, 72, 76 sts)

Foot

Work even in St st until foot measures approximately 5cm (2 inches) less than desired length.

Toe

Rnd 1: Knit to last 3 sts of needle 1, k2tog, k1; on needle 2, k1, ssk, knit to 3 sts from end, k2tog, k1; on needle 3, k1, ssk, knit to end.

Rnd 2: Knit around.

Rep Rnds 1 and 2 until 28 sts rem, ending with Rnd 1.

With needle 3, knit across sts of needle 1–14 sts on each of 2 needles.

Finishing

Cut yarn, leaving a 46-cm (18-inch) end. Weave toe using Kitchener method.

Three-Colour Tweed Socks

INTERMEDIATE

Size

Woman's small (medium, large, extra-large) instructions are given for smallest size, with larger sizes in parentheses. When only 1 number is given, it applies to all sizes.

Finished Measurement

Circumference: Approximately 19 (20.5, 23.5, 24.5)cm or 7½ (8, 9¼, 9¾) inches

Materials

- Brown Sheep Top of the Lamb 100 per cent wool sport weight yarn (141 metres (154 yds)/50g per skein): 2 (2, 2, 3) skeins deep forest #352 (MC), 1 skein each russet #200 (A), natural #100 (B)
- 3.25mm (size 3) set of double-pointed needles or size needed to obtain gauge
- Stitch markers

Gauge

13 sts and 18 rows = 5cm/2 inches in St st
To save time, take time to check gauge.

Pattern Stitch

Three-Colour Slip Stitch Tweed
(multiple of 3 sts)

Rnd 1: With A, *k2, sl 1 wyib; rep from * around.

Rnd 2: With A, *p2, sl 1 wyib; rep from * around.

Rnd 3: With B, k1, *sl 1 wyib, k2; rep from * to last 2 sts, end sl 1 wyib, k1.

Rnd 4: With B, p1, *sl 1 wyib, p2; rep from * to last 2 sts, end sl 1 wyib, p1.

Rnd 5: With MC, sl 1, *k2, sl 1 wyib; rep from * to last 2 sts, end k2.

Rnd 6: With MC, sl 1, *p2, sl 1 wyib; rep from * to last 2 sts, end p2.

Rep Rnds 1–6 for pat.

Pattern Note

Sl all sts purlwise, wyib.

Sock

With MC, cast on 48 (52, 60, 64) sts. Join without twisting, mark beg of rnd and work in k2, p2 ribbing until cuff measures 5cm (2 inches).

Purl 1 rnd, inc 0 (2, 0, 2) sts evenly. (48, 54, 60, 66 sts)

Work even in pat until cuff measures 19cm (7½ inches) or desired length from beg, ending with Rnd 6. Cut A and B.

Knit 1 rnd, dec 0 (2, 0, 2) sts evenly. (48, 52, 60, 64 sts)

Knit across 24 (26, 30, 32) sts with needle 1 (heel sts); divide rem sts so there are 12 (13, 15, 16) sts each on needles 2 and 3 (instep sts). Working on heel sts only, pm in centre of flap, after st 12 (13, 15, 16). Shaping will take place evenly on each side of marker.

Heel

Row 1 (WS): Sl 1, purl across.

Row 2: *Sl 1, k1; rep from * across.

Rep Rows 1 and 2 until there are 12 (13, 15, 16) lps on each edge of heel flap, ending with Row 2.

Turn heel
Row 1 (WS): Sl 1, p14 (15, 17, 18), p2tog, p1, turn.
Row 2: Sl 1, k5, k2tog, k1, turn.
Row 3: Sl 1, p6, p2tog, p1, turn.
Row 4: Sl 1, k7, k2tog, k1, turn.
Continue in this manner, working 1 more st before dec until all sts have been worked. (14, 16, 18, 18 sts)

Gusset
Needle 1: With needle containing heel sts, pick up and knit 12 (13, 15, 16) sts in lps along side of flap;
Needle 2: With free needle, knit 24 (26, 30, 32) instep sts onto 1 needle, *at the same time,* at each end, pick up either a st in row below, or twist running thread and knit it tog with first and last st;
Needle 3: With free needle, pick up and knit 12 (13, 15, 16) sts

in lps along other edge of heel flap, knit 7 (8, 9, 9) heel sts from needle 1 to needle 3. (62, 68, 78, 82 sts)
Rnd 1: Knit.
Rnd 2: Knit to last 3 sts on needle 1, k2tog, k1; knit across needle 2; on needle 3, k1, ssk, knit to end.
[Rep Rnds 1 and 2] 6 (7, 8, 8) times more. (48, 52, 60, 64 sts)

Foot
Work even in St st until foot

measures approximately 4.5cm (1¾ inches) less than desired length.

Toe
Rnd 1: Knit to last 3 sts of needle 1, k2tog, k1; on needle 2, k1, ssk, knit to last 3 sts, k2tog, k1; on needle 3, k1, ssk, knit to end.
Rnd 2: Knit.
Rep Rnds 1 and 2 until 28 sts rem, ending with Rnd 1.

   With needle 3, knit across sts of needle 1–14 sts on each of 2 needles.

Finishing
Cut yarn, leaving an 46-cm (18-inch) end. Weave toe using Kitchener method.

Stripes! Socks

INTERMEDIATE

Size
Woman's small (medium, large) instructions are given for smallest size, with larger sizes in parentheses. When only 1 number is given, it applies to all sizes.

Finished Measurement
Circumference: Approximately 18 (20.5, 23)cm or 7 (8, 9) inches

Materials

1 SUPER FINE

- Brown Sheep Wildfoote Luxury Sock Yarn 75 per cent washable wool/25 per cent nylon fingering weight yarn (197 metres (215 yds)/50g per skein): 2 skeins jungle #SY15 (MC), 1 skein each temple turquoise #SY19 (A), lullaby #SY34 (B)

- 2.25mm (size 1) double-pointed needles or size needed to obtain gauge
- Stitch markers

Gauge

16 sts and 19 rnds = 5cm/2 inches in St st (blocked)
To save time, take time to check your gauge.

Pattern Stitch

Stripe Sequence

Work in k2, p2 ribbing of *3 rnds B, 5 rnds A, 8 rnds MC, 5 rnds A; rep from * for desired length.

Sock

With MC, cast on 56 (64, 72) sts. Join without twisting, pm between first and last st.

Work in k2, p2 ribbing for 5cm (2 inches).

Beg stripe sequence and work until top measures 18 (20.5, 20.5)cm or 7 (8, 8) inches or desired length.

Cut A and B, work 2 rnds MC. Work rest of sock in MC.

Heel

Sl next 28 (32, 36) sts to 1 needle for heel, divide rem 28 (32, 36) sts between 2 needles for instep.

Working in rows on heel sts only, knit across.

Row 1 (WS): Sl 1, purl across.

Row 2: *Sl 1, k1; rep from * across.

Rep Rows 1 and 2 until there are 14 (16, 18) lps on each side of heel flap, ending with Row 2.

Turn heel

Row 1 (WS): Sl 1, p15 (17, 19), p2tog, p1, turn.

Row 2: Sl 1, k5, k2tog, k1, turn.

Row 3: Sl 1, p6, p2tog, p1, turn.

Row 4: Sl 1, k7, k2tog, k1, turn.

Row 5: Sl 1, p8, p2tog, p1, turn.

Row 6: Sl 1, k9, k2tog, k1, turn.

Continue in this manner, working 1 more st before dec each time, until all sts have been worked. (16, 18, 20 sts)

Gusset

Needle 1: Working along right edge of heel flap, pick up and knit 14 (16, 18) sts (1 st in each loop);

Needle 2: Work instep sts onto 1 needle, *at the same time*, at each end, pick up either a st in the row below, or twist the running thread and knit it tog with the first and last st;

Needle 3: Pick up and knit 14 (16, 18) sts along left edge of heel flap, then knit 8 (9, 10) heel sts from needle 1 to needle 3. There will be 22 (25, 28) sts on needles 1 and 3, and 28 (32, 36) sts on needle 2. (72, 82, 92 sts)

Rnd 1: Knit.

Rnd 2: Knit to last 3 sts of needle 1, k2tog, k1; knit sts of needle 2; on needle 3, k1, ssk, knit to end.

Rep Rnds 1 and 2 until needle 1 and needle 3 each contains 14 (16, 18) sts. (56, 64, 72 sts total)

Foot

Work even in St st until foot measures approximately 5cm (2 inches) less than desired length.

Toe

Rnd 1: Knit to last 3 sts of needle 1, k2tog, k1; on needle 2, k1, ssk, knit to last 3 sts, k2tog, k1; on needle 3, k1, ssk, knit to end.

Rnd 2: Knit.

Rep Rnds 1 and 2 until 28 sts rem, ending with Rnd 1.

With needle 3, knit across sts of needle 1. (14 sts on each of 2 needles)

Finishing

Cut yarn, leaving a 46-cm (18-inch) end. Weave toe using Kitchener method.

Wavy Rib Socks

INTERMEDIATE

Size

Child's extra-small (small, medium, large) instructions are given for smallest size, with larger sizes in parentheses. When only 1 number is given, it applies to all sizes.

Finished Measurement

Circumference: 13 (15, 17, 19)cm or 5¼ (6, 6¾, 7½) inches

Materials

- Brown Sheep Wildfoote Luxury Sock Yarn 75 per cent wool/25 per cent nylon fingering weight yarn (197 metres (215 yds)/50g per skein): 1 (1, 1, 2) skeins columbine #SY16 (MC), 1 skein each crystal pink #SY33 (A), vanilla #SY10 (B), little lilac #SY32 (C)

- 2.5mm (size 1) double-pointed needles, or size needed to obtain gauge
- Stitch markers

Gauge
16 sts and 19 rnds = 5cm/2 inches in St st (blocked)
To save time, take time to check your gauge.

Pattern Stitches
Wavy Ribs (multiple of 6 sts)
Rnds 1–4: K2, *p2, k4; rep from * to last 4 sts, p2, k2.
Rnds 5–8: P1, *k4, p2; rep from * to last 5 sts, k4, p1.
Rep Rnds 1–8 for pat.

Stripe Sequence
Work *5 rnds A, 6 rnds MC, 3 rnds B, 5 rnds C, 3 rnds B, 6 rnds MC; rep from * for stripe sequence.

Sock
With MC, cast on 40 (44, 52, 60) sts.

Join without twisting, pm between first and last st.

Work in k2, p2 ribbing until cuff measures 4cm (1½ inches).

Purl 1 rnd, knit 1 rnd inc 2 (4, 2, 0) sts evenly. (42, 48, 54, 60 sts)

Beg with A, work in pat and stripe sequence until top measures 12 (14, 15, 16.5)cm or 4¾ (5½, 6, 6½) inches or desired length from beg.

Cut all CC, work rem of sock with MC only.

Knit 1 rnd, dec 2 (0, 2, 0) sts evenly. (40, 48, 52, 60 sts)

Knit next rnd, ending 10 (12, 13, 15) sts before end of rnd.

Knit next 20 (24, 26, 30) sts onto 1 needle for heel, divide rem 20 (24, 26, 30) sts between 2 needles and leave for instep.

Heel

Working on heel sts only, turn.
Row 1 (WS): Sl 1, purl across.
Row 2: *Sl 1, k1; rep from *
across.
Rep Rows 1 and 2 until there are
10 (12, 13, 15) lps on each side of
heel flap, ending with a RS row
and pm for centre of heel after st
#10 (12, 13, 15).

Shaping is evenly spaced on
each side of marker.

Turn heel

Row 1: Sl 1, p11 (13, 14, 16),
p2tog, p1, turn.
Row 2: Sl 1, k5, k2tog, k1, turn.
Row 3: Sl 1, p6, p2tog, p1, turn.
Row 4: Sl 1, k7, k2tog, k1, turn.
Continue in this manner,
working 1 more st before dec
each time until all sts have been
worked. (12, 14, 16, 18 sts)

Gusset

Needle 1: With needle
containing heel sts, pick up
and knit 10 (12, 13, 15) sts in lps
along edge of heel flap;
Needle 2: Work 20 (24, 26, 30)
instep sts onto 1 needle, *at the
same time,* at each end, pick
up either a st in row below, or
twist running thread and knit
it tog with first and last st; with
3rd needle, pick up and knit 10
(12, 13, 15) sts in lps along other
edge of heel flap, knit 6 (7, 8, 9)
heel sts from needle 1 to needle
3. (52, 62, 68, 78 sts)
Rnd 1: Knit.
Rnd 2: Knit to last 3 sts on
needle 1, k2tog, k1; knit across
needle 2; on needle 3, k1, ssk,
knit to end.
[Rep Rnds 1 and 2] 5 (6, 7,8)
times more. (40, 48, 52, 60 sts)

Work even until foot
measures 12.5 (14, 15, 18)cm
or 5 (5½, 6, 7) inches or
approximately 4.5cm (1¾ inches)
less than desired length.

Toe

Rnd 1: Knit to last 3 sts of needle
1, k2tog, k1; on needle 2, k1, ssk,
knit to last 3 sts, k2tog, k1; on
needle 3, k1, ssk, knit to end.
Rnd 2: Knit.
Rep Rnds 1 and 2 until 24 sts
rem, ending with Rnd 1.

With needle 3, knit across sts
of needle 1. (12 sts on each of 2
needles)

Finishing

Cut yarn, leaving a 46-cm
(18-inch) end. Weave toe using
Kitchener method. ◆

Little Royalty Bibs

Precious princess and prince babies deserve a royal knitted-bib treatment.

DESIGN BY MEGAN LACEY

EASY

Finished Size
Approximately 20.5 x 25.5cm (8 x 10 inches)

Materials
- Bernat Cottontots 100 per cent worsted weight cotton yarn (156 metres (171 yds)/100g per ball): 1 ball each little boy blue #90128 (A) and blue berry #90129 (B) for boy's version; 1 ball each pretty in pink #90420 (C) and strawberry #90421 (D) for girl's version
- 4.5mm (size 7) needles or size needed to obtain gauge
- 6.5 sq cm (1 inch square) of hook-and-loop tape

Gauge
20 sts and 26 rows = 10cm/4 inches in St st
To save time, take time to check gauge.

Special Abbreviation
M1 (Make 1): Inc by k1 in back of strand between st just worked and next st on LH needle.

Bib
With A (C), cast on 18 sts.
Row 1 (RS): K1, M1, knit to last st, M1, k1. (20 sts)

Row 2 (WS): Purl across.
Rows 3–14: [Rep Rows 1 and 2] 6 times. (32 sts)
Continue to work in St st until bib measures 12.5cm (5 inches) from cast-on edge, ending with a WS row.

Left side
Row 1 (RS): K10, turn, leaving rem sts for later.
Row 2 and all WS rows: Purl across.
Row 3: K7, k2tog, k1. (9 sts)
Row 5: K6, k2tog, k1. (8 sts)
Continue to work in St st on rem sts until strap measures 12.5cm (5 inches), ending with a WS row.

Shape end
Row 1 (RS): K2, ssk, k2tog, k2. (6 sts)
Rows 2 and 4: Purl across.
Row 3: K1, ssk, k2tog, k1. (4 sts)
Bind off rem sts.

Right side
With RS facing, join yarn to rem 22 sts.
Row 1: Bind off first 12 sts for neckline, knit to end of row.
Row 2 and all WS rows: Purl across.
Row 3: K1, ssk, k7. (9 sts)

Row 5: K1, ssk, k6. (8 sts)
Continue to work in St st on rem sts until strap measures 12.5cm (5 inches), ending with a WS row.
Shape end as for left side.

Crown
With B (D), cast on 11 sts.
Rows 1–4: Knit.
Rows 5–10: Beg with a RS row, work 6 rows in St st.

First point
Row 11 (RS): K3, turn.
Rows 12 and 14: P3.
Row 13: K3.
Row 15: Sl 1, k2tog, psso, fasten off.

Centre point
With RS facing, attach yarn to rem 8 sts.
Row 11 (RS): K5, turn.
Rows 12 and 14: P5.
Row 13: K5.
Row 15: Ssk, k1, k2tog. (3 sts)
Row 16: P3.
Row 17: Sl 1, k2tog, psso, fasten off.

Last point
With RS facing, attach yarn to rem 3 sts and work as for first point.

Finishing
Outside edge trim
With B (D), RS facing, pick up and knit 100 sts around outside edge of bib. Knit 1 row on WS. Bind off all sts.

Neck trim
With B (D), RS facing, pick up and knit 56 sts around neck edge of bib, beg and ending at beg and end of outside edge trim. Knit 1 row on WS. Bind off all sts.

Sew crown on centre front of bib. Sew hook-and-loop tape to strap ends, making sure that pieces are sewn on WS of 1 strap and RS of other strap. Lay bib flat and block with a damp cloth. ◆

Log Cabin Baby Blanket

The traditional quilt pattern Log Cabin inspired this cosy blanket. Soft shades are combined with white to achieve the impression of printed cloth.

DESIGN BY DIANE ZANGL

EASY

Size
Approximately 101.5 x 101.5cm (40 x 40 inches)

Materials

- Plymouth Dreambaby DK 50 per cent nylon/50 per cent microfibre acrylic DK weight yarn (167 metres (183 yds)/50g per ball): 6 balls each baby pink #119 and white #100, 7 balls baby blue #102
- 5.5mm (size 9) 73.5-cm or 29-inch circular needle or size needed to obtain gauge
- Stitch marker

Gauge
16 sts and 32 rows (16 ridges) = 10cm/4 inches in garter st
To save time, take time to check gauge.

Colour Sequence
Work 2 blocks each of pink, pink/white, blue, and then blue/white.

Pattern Notes
Two strands of yarn are held tog for entire blanket.

Always give piece a ¼ turn clockwise before picking up sts for next section. With RS facing, pick up sts between ridges along side edge of block and in front strand of bound-off sts.

You will always have a multiple of 8 sts on the needle.

Using a separate strand of yarn to pick up sts for the I-cord edging prevents the unwanted 'blip' of another colour showing through the edging.

Diagram shows colour placement and direction of work for first 3 full rounds of blocks. Continue with following blocks in same manner.

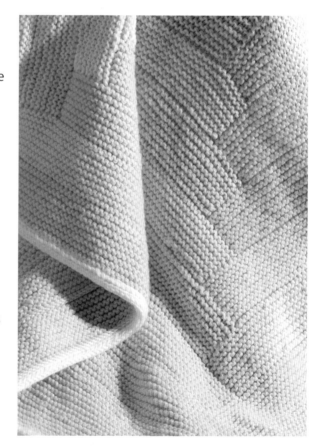

Blanket
Block 1
With 2 strands of pink held tog, cast on 8 sts. Knit 15 rows (8 ridges on RS). Mark RS of this square. Bind off, leaving last st on needle.

Give square a ¼ turn clockwise.

Block 2

Cut 1 strand pink, join white. Pick up and knit 7 sts along side of first block. Knit 15 rows. Bind off, leaving last st on needle.

Give square a ¼ turn clockwise.

Block 3

Pick up and knit 7 sts along side edge of last block and 8 sts along cast-on edge of Block 1. (16 sts)

Knit 15 rows. Bind off, leaving last st on needle.

Give square a ¼ turn clockwise.

Block 4

Cut yarn, join 2 strands blue. Pick up and knit 16 sts along side edge of last block. (16 sts)

Knit 15 rows. Bind off, leaving last st on needle.

Give square a ¼ turn clockwise.

Block 5

Pick up and knit 23 sts along side edge of last block. (24 sts)

Knit 15 rows. Bind off, leaving last st on needle.

Give square a ¼ turn clockwise.

Block 6

Cut 1 strand blue, join 1 strand white. Pick up and knit 23 sts along side edge of last block. (24 sts)

Knit 15 rows. Bind off, leaving last st on needle.

Give square a ¼ turn clockwise.

Block 7

Pick up and knit 31 sts along side edge of last block. (32 sts)

Knit 15 rows. Bind off, leaving last st on needle.

Give square a ¼ turn clockwise.

Maintaining colour sequence, continue to work in this manner, adding a new block onto those previously worked until blanket measures approximately 258 sq cm (40 inches square).

Bind off all sts of last block (last block will have 160 sts).

I-cord Edging

With 2 strands of white held tog, pick up and knit 1 st in each bound-off stitch of last row.

Drop yarn, do not cut. Return to first picked-up st and with separate double strand of white, cast on 4 sts to LH needle.

*K3, ssk (cord st along with picked-up st), sl sts just worked back to LH needle. Rep from * until all picked-up sts have been worked.

Return to first double strand of yarn. Pick up and knit along 2nd side of blanket. Continue edging until all picked-up sts along 2nd side have been worked. Rep for rem 2 sides.

Cut yarn and weave final sts to cast-on sts of edging. Hide ends in edging. ◆

```
KEY
#1 etc  = Order of work
─→  = Direction of work
B = Blue
P = Pink
W = White
BW = Blue & white
PW = Pink & white
```

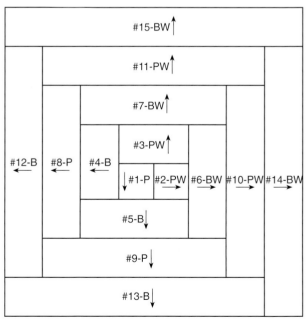

LOG CABIN DIAGRAM

Plain & Fancy Christening Blanket

A textured lace blanket in a wide range of sizes will make that special day even more extraordinary.

DESIGN BY PAULINE SCHULTZ

EASY

Size
Cot size (small, medium, large) instructions are given for smallest size, with larger sizes in parentheses. When only 1 number is given, it applies to all sizes.

Finished Measurements
Approximately 76 x 101.5 (101.5 x 127, 114.5 x 152, 127 x 178)cm or 30 x 40 (40 x 50, 45 x 60, 50 x 70) inches

Materials
- Plymouth Dreambaby DK 50 per cent microfibre acrylic/50 per cent nylon DK weight yarn (167 metres (183 yds)/50g per ball): 6 (10, 12, 16) balls white #100
- 4mm (size 6) 81.5-cm (32-inch) circular needle or size needed to obtain gauge

Gauge
22 sts and 9 rows = 10cm/4 inches in Lace Diamonds pat
To save time, take time to check gauge.

Pattern Stitch
Lace Diamonds
Row 1 (RS): Knit.
Row 2 and all WS rows: Knit.
Row 3: K3, *k4, k2tog, yo twice, k2tog, k4; rep from * to last 3 sts, k3.
Row 5: K3, *k2, [k2tog, yo twice, k2tog] twice, k2; rep from * to last 3 sts, k3.
Row 7: K3, *k2tog, yo twice, k2tog; rep from * to last 3 sts, k3.
Row 9: Rep Row 5.
Row 11: Rep Row 3.
Row 13: Knit.
Row 15: K3, *yo, k2tog, k8, k2tog, yo; rep from * to last 3 sts, k3.
Row 17: K3, k2tog, yo twice, k2tog, k4, *[K2tog, yo twice, k2tog] twice, k4; rep from * to last 7 sts, k2tog, yo twice, k2tog, k3.
Row 19: K3, yo, k2tog, *k2tog, yo twice, k2tog; rep from * to last 5 sts, k2tog, yo, k3.

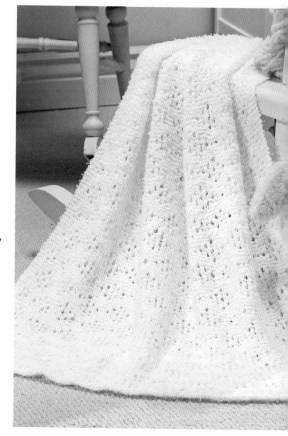

Row 21: Rep Row 17.
Row 23: Rep Row 15.
Row 24: Rep Row 2.
Rep Rows 1–24 for pat.

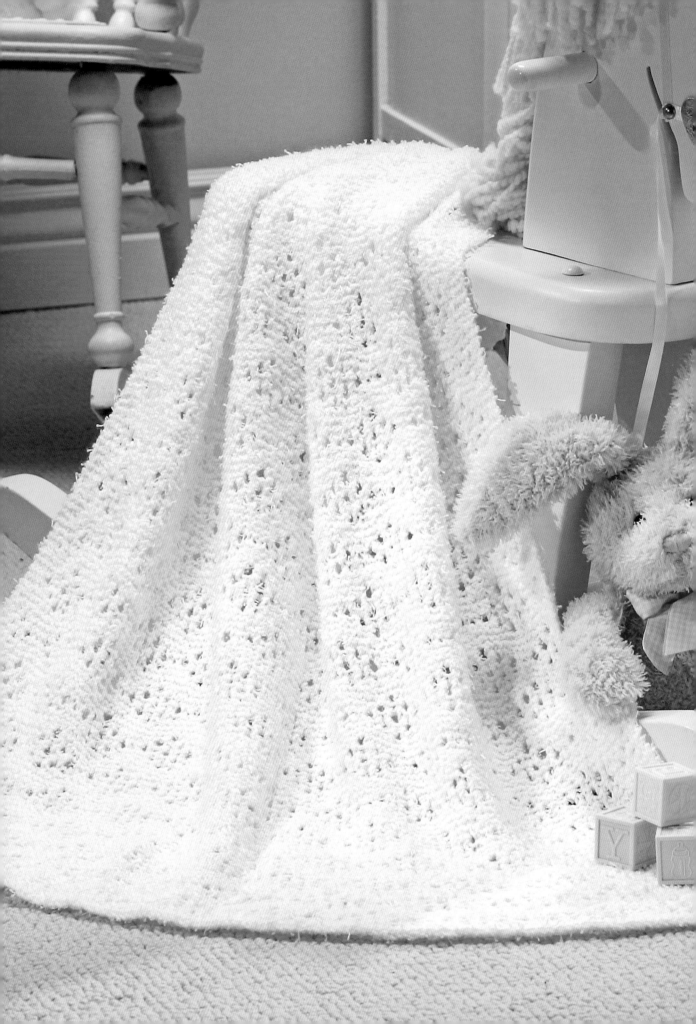

Pattern Notes

Circular needle is used to accommodate large number of sts. Do not join; work in rows.

Knit all WS rows, working double yo as k1, p1, and single yo as k1.

Afghan blooms by about 15 per cent when washed and blocked.

When joining a new skein of yarn, knit 2 strands tog for 4–5 sts. The slightly heavier sts won't be noticed in overall texture.

Trim ends after washing and blocking.

Blanket

Cast on 150 (198, 222, 258) sts.
Knit 2 rows.

Referring to chart or written pat, work even until blanket measures approximately 86.5 (109, 130, 152)cm or 34 (43, 51, 60) inches, ending with Row 12 or 24 of pat.

Knit 4 rows.
Bind off knitwise. ✦

PLAIN & FANCY CHART
Note: Only RS rows are shown. Knit on all WS rows.

STITCH KEY
☐ Knit
◉ Yo
⟋ K2tog

Dragonflies

Sweet dreams are sure to abound while these magical, wispy creatures fly about.

DESIGN BY KATHY SASSER

EASY

Finished Size
Approximately 96.5 x 114.5cm
(38 x 45 inches)

Materials

MEDIUM
- Plymouth Encore
  Worsted 75 per cent
  acrylic/25 per cent wool
  worsted weight yarn (183
  metres (200 yds)/100g per
  ball): 4 balls white #208 (MC),
  3 balls mint #1201 (CC)
- 4.5mm (size 7) 61-cm (24-inch)
  circular needle or size needed
  to obtain gauge
- Stitch markers

Gauge
19 sts and 26 rows = 10cm/4
inches in St st
To save time, take time to check
gauge.

Special Abbreviations
3-Yo: Wrap yarn around needle
3 times.
4-Yo: Wrap yarn around needle
4 times.
5-Yo: Wrap yarn around needle
5 times.

Square Knot
A square knot is formed by
using 2 single knots. Bring the
right lp over, then under the
left lp and pull up securely and
in opposite directions. Next,
bring the now left lp over, then
under the right lp and again pull
securely in opposite directions
until a snug knot is formed
between the lps.

Pattern Stitch
Dragonfly
Rows 1–4: Knit.
Row 5 (WS): K5, *5-Yo, k1, 5-Yo,
k9; rep from *, end last rep k5.
Row 6: Knit, slipping all 5-Yo lps
from LH needle and pushing to
front without working. Insert
RH needle into each pair of
lps (1 pair at a time) and pull
up snugly, holding thumb and
forefinger of left hand at base
of lps, to take slack out of sts
between and on either side of
pair of lps. Tie each pair of lps
into a firm square knot.
Rows 7–12: Knit.
Row 13 (WS): K5, *3-Yo, k1,
3-Throw, k9; rep from *, end last
rep k5.
Row 14: Knit, slipping all 3-Yo
lps from left needle, and pulling
up snugly with free needle as
in Row 6. Before tying, separate
each pair of lps and bring the
5-Yo lps up towards the needle.
Then tie the 3-Yo lps over them
with a firm square knot. This
forms the body and lower wings.
Row 15 (WS): K5, *4-Yo, k1, 4-Yo,
k9; rep from *, end last rep k5.
Row 16: Knit across row,
slipping all 4-Yo lps from left
needle and pulling up snugly as
in Row 6. Before tying, separate
each pair of lps, lay upper body
of dragonfly across these and tie
this last pair of lps across body
in a firm square knot. This forms
the head and upper wings.
Rows 17–22: Knit.
    Rep Rows 1–22 for pat.

Colour Stripe Sequence
Work in St st and colour
sequence of 17 rows MC, 2
rows CC.

Pattern Notes

Circular needle is used to accommodate large number of sts. Do not join; work in rows.

Wind separate balls or bobbins for each side border.

To avoid holes when changing colours, always bring new colour up over old.

Dragonfly motifs are worked at random in duplicate st after blanket is complete.

Blanket

With CC, cast on 181 sts. Work 22 rows of Dragonflies pat.

Set up pat:

Next row (WS): With CC, work 11 sts in Dragonfly pat, pm, p159 MC, pm, join 2nd ball of CC and work 11 sts in Dragonfly pat.

Keeping 11 sts at each end in established Dragonfly pat and rem sts in Colour Stripe sequence, work even until 14 white stripes have been completed. Cut MC. (264 rows)
Next row (WS): With CC, k11, purl to last 11 sts, k11.

Beg with Row 2 of Dragonfly pat, work across all sts until Row 22 is complete.

Bind off loosely.

Embroidery

Referring to charts, embroider dragonflies with CC in duplicate st, scattering motifs in a random pat. ✦

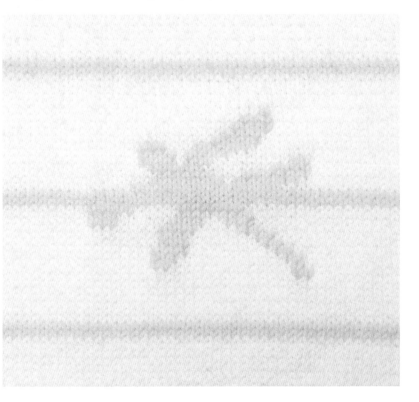

COLOUR KEY
□ MC
■ CC

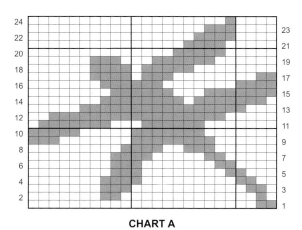

CHART A

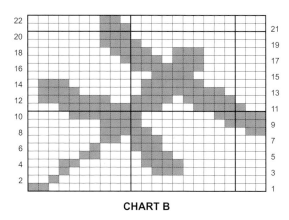

CHART B

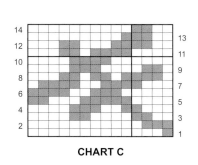

CHART C

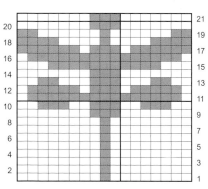

CHART D

Candy Rainbow Baby Afghan

This simple afghan uses only knit and purl stitches. Its rainbow of colour will attract the eye of your little one.

DESIGN BY NAZANIN S FARD

BEGINNER

Finished Size
Approximately 101.5 x 101.5cm (40 x 40 inches)

Materials
- Coats & Clark Red Heart Baby Econo Pompadour 90 per cent acrylic/10 per cent polypropylene yarn (421 metres (460 yds)/170g): 3 skeins candy print #1047
- 4mm (size 6) needles or size needed to obtain gauge
- Tapestry needle
- 4mm (size G/6) crochet hook

Gauge
20 sts and 27 rows = 10cm/4 inches in St st
To save time, take time to check gauge.

Pattern Stitch
(multiple of 20 sts + 2)
Rows 1, 3, 5, 7, 9 and 11 (RS): P1, *[k2, p2] twice, k2, [p1, k1] 5 times; rep from *, end p1.
Rows 2, 4, 6, 8, 10 and 12: K1, *[k1, p1] 5 times, [p2, k2] twice, p2; rep from *, end k1.
Rows 13, 15, 17, 19, 21 and 23: P1, *[k1, p1] 5 times, [k2, p2] twice, k2; rep from *, end p1.
Rows 14, 16, 18, 20, 22 and 24: K1, *[p2, k2] twice, p2, [p1, k1] 5 times; rep from *, end k1.
Rep Rows 1–24 for pat.

Afghan Strips
Make 4
Cast on 62 sts. Work in pat until piece meas 101.5cm (40 inches). Bind off loosely.

Finishing
Sew strips side by side. Crochet 1 rnd of sc around edges. Turn and work rnd of reverse sc (crab stitch) around. Fasten off. ◆

Baby Rainbow

Bright rainbow colours combine with a variation of the Old Shale pattern in a delightful baby afghan.

DESIGN BY LYNDA ROPER

EASY

Finished Size
Approximately 76 x 101.5cm (30 x 40 inches)

Materials

- Plymouth Encore Worsted 75 per cent acrylic/25 per cent wool worsted weight yarn (183 metres (200 yds)/100g per ball): 1 ball each purple #1384, red #1386, orange #1383, yellow #1382, green #54, royal blue #133
- 5.5mm (size 9) straight needles or size needed to obtain gauge

Gauge
17 sts and 24 rows = 10cm/4 inches in pat st
To save time, take time to check gauge.

Pattern Stitch
Rainbow
Row 1 (RS): K2, [k2tog] twice, *[yo, k1] 4 times, [k2tog] 4 times; rep from * to last 10 sts, [yo, k1] 4 times, [k2tog] twice, k2.
Row 2: K2, purl to last 2 sts, k2. Join next colour.
Rows 3 and 4: Knit.
Rep Rows 1–4 for pat.

Colour Sequence
Work 4 rows of pat, changing colours after Row 2 in rainbow order of purple, red, orange, yellow, green, blue.

Afghan
With purple, cast on 124 sts.
  Knit 2 rows.
  Work Rows 1–2 of pat, change to red.

Work even in pat and colour sequence until 8 sets of colours have been completed, ending with blue Row 2. Join purple.
  Rep Rows 3–4, then Row 1.
  Knit 1 row.
  Bind off knitwise on RS. ◆

Seeing Stars

Tiny stars abound on a colourful lap robe. The size also makes it suitable for a child.

DESIGN BY JOYCE ENGLUND

EASY

Finished Size
Approximately 86.5 x 112cm
(34 x 44 inches)

Materials
- Plymouth Encore
  Worsted 75 per cent acrylic/25
  per cent wool worsted weight
  yarn (183 metres (200 yds)/100g
  per ball): 3 balls each off-white
  #146 (MC), turquoise #235 (A)
  and gold #1014 (B)
- 6mm (size 10) 79-cm (30-inch)
  circular needle or size needed
  to obtain gauge
- Stitch markers

Gauge
19 sts and 22 rows = 10cm/4
inches in Star pat
To save time, take time to check
gauge.

Special Abbreviations
Make Star: P3tog leaving sts on
needle, yo, then purl same 3 sts
tog again.

M1 (Make 1): Make a backward
lp and place on RH needle.

Pattern Stitches
A. Seed
Row 1: K1, *p1, k1; rep from *
across.
All following rows: Knit the purl
sts and purl the knit sts as they
present themselves.

B. Star (multiple of 4 sts + 1)
Rows 1 and 3 (RS): Knit.
Row 2: P1, Make Star, p1; rep
from * across.
Row 4: P3, Make Star, *p1, Make
Star; rep from * to last 3 sts, p3.
Rep Rows 1–4 for pat.

C. Colour Sequence
Work 2 rows each of A, B, A, MC,
B, A, B, MC.

Pattern Notes
Circular needle is used to
accommodate large number
of sts. Do not join; work in rows.

Lap Robe
With MC, cast on 151 sts.
   Work in Seed pat for 8 rows.
Inc row (WS): Work 6 sts in Seed
pat, pm, k1, M1, *k2, M1; rep
from * to last 6 sts, pm, work 6 sts
in Seed pat.

   Keeping first and last 6 sts in
MC and Seed pat, and rem sts in
Star pat and colour sequence,
work even until lap robe
measures approximately 108cm
(42½ inches), ending with A and
Row 3 of pat.
Dec row (WS): With MC, work 6
sts in Seed pat, remove marker,
*p1, p2tog; rep from * to last 7
sts, k1, remove marker, work 6 sts
in Seed pat.
   Work 8 rows of Seed pat.
   Bind off in pat. ◆

Lilacs in Bloom

Wrap a baby in luxury with a cuddly alpaca afghan in a soft lilac shade. An added bonus—it's reversible.

DESIGN BY SHARI HAUX

BEGINNER

Finished Size
Approximately 109 x 109cm (43 x 43 inches)

Materials
- Plymouth Baby Alpaca Grande 100 per cent superfine baby alpaca bulky weight yarn (101 metres (110 yds/100g per skein): 8 skeins lavender #1830
- 8mm (size 11) 61-cm (24-inch) circular needle or size needed to obtain gauge
- Stitch markers

Gauge
12 sts and 16 rows = 10cm/4 inches in Tiny Block pat
To save time, take time to check gauge.

Pattern Stitch
Tiny Blocks
Rows 1 and 2: *K2, p2; rep from * across.
Rows 3 and 4: *P2, k2; rep from * across.
Rep Rows 1–4 for pat.

Afghan
Cast on 116 sts.
    Work in garter st for 10 rows.

Set up pat:
K10, pm, work in Tiny Blocks pat to last 10 sts, pm, k10.
    Keeping sts between markers in Tiny Blocks pat and rem sts in garter st, work even until afghan measures approximately 104cm (41

inches), ending with Row 2 or 4 of pat.
    Knit 10 rows.
    Bind off. ◆

Rainbow Squares

The joining seams of easy-knit blocks form an integral part of the design in a colourful afghan.

DESIGN BY SCARLET TAYLOR

BEGINNER

Finished Size
Approximately 160 x 106.5cm (63 x 42 inches) (excluding fringe)

Materials

SUPER BULKY

- Plymouth Rimini Rainbow 60 per cent acrylic/40 per cent wool super bulky weight yarn (35 metres (38 yds)/50g per ball): 26 balls fruit rainbow #10
- 9mm (size 13) needles or size needed to obtain gauge
- 8mm (size L/11) crochet hook
- Matching worsted weight yarn for seaming

Gauge
8 sts and 12 rows = 10cm/4 inches in St st
To save time, take time to check gauge.

Afghan
Basic Square
Make 24
Cast on 21 sts.

Work in St st until square measures 26.5cm (10½ inches), ending with a WS row. Bind off loosely.

Assembly
Lay out squares in 6 rows of 4 blocks each to form a pleasing pat.

With RS facing and matching worsted weight yarn, backstitch 6 squares tog, creating a reverse seam.

Join strips in same manner with long vertical seams.

Cut strands of yarn, each 35.5cm (14 inches) long.

Holding 3 strands tog, fold each group in half.

Working along sides of 1 square, insert crochet hook from WS to RS.

Pull fold of fringe through fabric. Draw ends through lp and fasten tightly.

Having 6 fringes along each side of each square, rep around

all 4 sides of afghan.
Trim fringe evenly. ◆

Mirror Image

No more trying to figure out which side is the right side. It's reversible!

DESIGN BY KATHLEEN SASSER

EASY

Finished Size
Approximately 112 x 142cm (44 x 56 inches)

Materials
- Plymouth Galway Worsted 100 per cent wool worsted weight yarn (192 metres (210 yds)/100g per ball): 10 balls light blue aqua #128
- 4.5mm (size 7) 91.5-cm (36-inch) circular needle or size needed to obtain gauge
- Stitch markers

Gauge
19 sts and 23 rows = 10cm/4 inches in Moss Diamond pat
To save time, take time to check gauge.

Pattern Stitches
A. Double Moss
Rows 1 and 2: *K1, p1; rep from * across.
Rows 3 and 4: *P1, k1; rep from * across.
Rep Rows 1–4 for pat.

B. Moss Diamond (multiple of 24 sts)
Rows 1 and 2: *K6, p6; rep from * across.
Rows 3 and 4: *P1, k5, p5, k1; rep from * across.

Rows 5 and 6: *K1, p1, k4, p4, k1, p1; rep from * across.
Rows 7 and 8: *P1, k1, p1, k3, p3, k1, p1, k1; rep from * across.
Rows 9 and 10: *[K1, p1] twice, k2, p2, [k1, p1] twice; rep from * across.
Rows 11 and 12: *P1, k1; rep from * across.
Rows 13 and 14: *K1, p1; rep from * across.
Rows 15 and 16: *[P1, k1] twice, p2, k2, [p1, k1] twice; rep from * across.
Rows 17 and 18: *K1, p1, k1, p3, k3, p1, k1, p1; rep from * across.
Rows 19 and 20: *P1, k1, p4, k4, p1, k1; rep from * across.
Rows 21 and 22: *K1, p5, k5, p1; rep from * across.
Rows 23 and 24: *P6, k6; rep from * across.
Rows 25 and 26: *P5, k1, p1, k5; rep from * across.
Rows 27 and 28: *P4, [k1, p1] twice, k4; rep from * across.
Rows 29 and 30: *P3, [k1, p1] 3 times, k3; rep from * across.
Rows 31 and 32: *P2, [k1, p1] 4 times, k2; rep from * across.
Rows 33 and 34: *P1, k1; rep from * across.
Rows 35 and 36: *K1, p1; rep from * across.
Rows 37 and 38: *K2, [p1, k1] 4 times, p2; rep from * across.

Rows 39 and 40: *K3, [p1, k1] 3 times, p3; rep from * across.
Rows 41 and 42: *K4, [p1, k1] twice, p4; rep from * across.
Rows 43 and 44: *K5, p1, k1, p5; rep from * across.
Rep Rows 1–44 for pat.

Pattern Notes
Circular needle is used to accommodate large number of sts.

Do not join; work in rows.

Throw
Cast on 212 sts.

Work in Double Moss pattern for 5cm (2 inches).

Set up pat
Work 10 sts in Double Moss pat, pm, work in Moss Diamond pat to last 10 sts, pm, work 10 sts in Double Moss pat.

Work even in established pats, until 7 reps of Moss Diamond pat have been completed.

Removing markers, work Double Moss pattern across all stitches for 5cm (2 inches).

Bind off in pat. ◆

Seaside Throw

With gorgeous yarn and a little time, you'll soon be enjoying this reversible throw.

DESIGN BY SCARLET TAYLOR

BEGINNER

Finished Measurements
Approximately 112 x 140cm
(44 x 55 inches)

Materials

- N.Y. Yarns Action 70
  per cent acrylic/30 per cent
  bulky weight wool yarn (45
  metres (49 yds)/50g per ball):
  22 balls cool #4
- 9mm (size 13) circular knitting
  needle or size needed to
  obtain gauge.
- Large crochet hook (for fringe)

Gauge
9 sts and 14 rows = 10cm/4 inches
in K3, p3 rib
To save time, take time to check
gauge.

Pattern Notes
Circular needle is used to
accommodate large number
of sts.
 Do not join; work back and
forth in rows.

Throw
Loosely cast on 99 sts.
Row 1 (RS): K3, *p3, k3; rep from
* across.
Row 2: P3, *k3, p3; rep from *
across.
 Rep Rows 1 and 2 for pat until
throw measures approximately
140cm (55 inches) from beg,
ending with a WS row.
 Bind off loosely in rib.
 Block lightly if desired.

Fringe
Make Single Knot fringe,
referring to page 8. Cut 35.5-cm
(14-inch) strands for fringe.
Use 3 strands for each knot;
tie a knot at end of each k3
rib across RS of cast-on and
bound-off edges. Trim ends
even. ✦

Wrapped in Ripples

Here is a knit variation of the favourite crochet ripple afghan.

DESIGN BY LOIS S YOUNG

EASY

Size
Approximately 109 x 135cm
(43 x 53 inches)

Materials

- Brown Sheep Lamb's Pride Worsted, 85 per cent wool/15 per cent mohair worsted weight yarn (174 metres (190 yds)/113g per skein): 4 skeins blue flannel #M82 (A), 3 skeins each white frost #M11 (B), lotus pink #M38 (C) and blue boy #M79 (D)
- 9mm (size 13) 81-cm (32-inch) circular needle or size needed to obtain gauge

Gauge
17 stitches and 8 rows = 10cm/4 inches in pat
To save time, take time to check gauge.

Pattern Stitch
Ripples
Row 1 (RS): Sl 1, k1, *(k1, [yo, k1] twice) in same st, [ssk] 3 times, sl 2, k1, p2sso, [k2tog] 3 times, (k1, [yo, k1] twice) in same st; rep from * across, end last rep k2.

Row 2: Sl 1, k1, purl to last 2 sts, k2.
Rep Rows 1–2 for pat.

Pattern Notes
Two strands of yarn are held tog for entire afghan.

Circular needle is used to accommodate large number of stitches. Do not join; work in rows.

Slip first st of each row knitwise.

Colour sequence:
Work 2 rows each of B, C, D and A.

Afghan
With A, cast on 191 sts loosely.

Work Rows 1 and 2 of Ripples pat, rep Row 1.
Next row: Sl 1, knit to end of row.

Work in colour sequence for 13 reps, ending with Row 1 of colour A.
Next row: Sl 1, knit to end of row.

Rep Row 1.
Bind off knitwise on WS.

Side Border
With RS facing, pick up and knit 1 st in each row along side edge.

Knit 2 rows, slipping first st of each row knitwise.

Bind off knitwise on WS.

Rep border along 2nd edge.

Block, pinning out points at both ends. ✦

Rainbow Fiesta

This cosy afghan is easy enough for the newest knitter!

DESIGN BY BONNIE FRANZ

BEGINNER

Finished Size
Approximately 124.5 x 152cm (49 x 60 inches)

Materials

SUPER BULKY

• Plymouth Rimini Rainbow 60 per cent acrylic/40 per cent wool super bulky weight yarn (35 metres (38 yds)/50g per ball): 13 balls fiesta #19
• 10mm (size 15) 61-cm (24-inch) circular needle or size needed to obtain gauge

Gauge
5 sts and 9 rows = 10cm/4 inches in pat
To save time, take time to check gauge.

Pattern Note
The pattern in this afghan (look at the photo for reference) is formed at the very end by dropping stitches all the way down from the top to the bottom when binding off, forming the ladders you see in the photo.

Afghan
Cast on 59 sts.
    Work even in St st until

afghan measures152cm (60 inches), ending with a WS row.
Drop st bind-off row: *Bind off 4 sts in the regular fashion, then drop the next st from the left hand needle. This stitch will be unravelled from top to bottom. **Note:** *Wait to completely unravel each dropped stitch until you've completed all bind offs. Only unravel them a few rows down to begin with.*

Drop the first one down about 5 rows.
    The fabric spreads out when the stitch is undone. To compensate for the fabric spread and maintain the width across the top, [cast on 1 st and immediately bind it off] 3 times (making a chain across the top of the widest unravelled stitch); rep from * to last 4 sts, bind off 4 sts. ◆

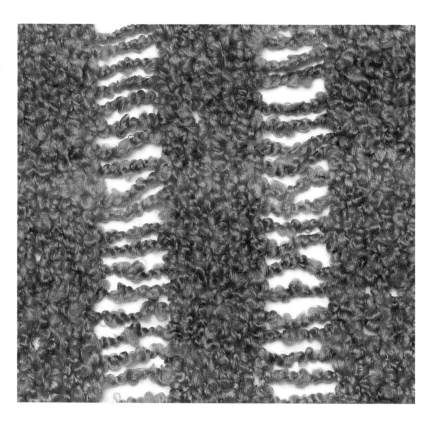

Walkabout Throw

Desert colours are reminiscent of the Australian Outback in this effortless fringed throw.

DESIGN BY MELISSA LEAPMAN

EASY

Finished Size
Approximately 117 x 137cm or 46 x 54 inches (excluding fringe)

Materials
- Plymouth Outback Wool 100 per cent virgin wool worsted weight yarn (338 metres (370 yds)/200g per skein): 5 skeins Southwest print #995
- 5mm (size 8) 91.5-cm (36-inch) circular needle or size needed to obtain gauge
- 5.5mm (size I/9) crochet hook

Gauge
18 sts and 26 rows = 10cm/4 inches in Walkabout pat
To save time, take time to check gauge.

Pattern Stitch
Walkabout (multiple of 7 sts + 4)
Row 1 (RS): K4, *yo, sl next st purlwise, k2tog, psso, yo, k4; rep from * across row.
Rows 2 and 3: Knit.
Row 4: Purl.
Rep Rows 1–4 for pat.

Pattern Notes
Circular needle is used to accommodate large number of sts.

Do not join; work in rows.

Throw
Cast on 207 sts.

Work even in Walkabout pat until throw measures approximately 137cm (54 inches), ending with Row 2 of pat.

Bind off knitwise.

Fringe
Cut strands of yarn, each 30.5cm (12 inches) long.

Holding 7 strands tog, fold each group in half.

Working along cast-on edge, insert crochet hook from WS to RS of k4 section. Pull fold of fringe through fabric. Draw ends through lp and fasten tightly.

Rep fringe in each k4 section. Rep along bound-off edge. Trim fringe evenly. ◆

Student's Throw

Knit a throw for your favourite student. Easy garter stitch, large needles and textured yarns combine for a project that will be finished in no time.

DESIGN BY ANITA CLOSIC

BEGINNER

Size
Approximately 114.5 x 140cm (45 x 55 inches)

Materials

- Plymouth Encore Worsted 75 per cent acrylic/25 per cent wool worsted weight yarn (183 metres (200 yds)/100g per skein): 6 balls olive #45 (A)
- Plymouth Rimini Rainbow 60 per cent acrylic/40 per cent wool super bulky weight yarn (35 metres (38 yds)/50g per ball): 10 balls brown rainbow #29 (B)
- Plymouth Hand Paint Wool 100 per cent wool super bulky weight yarn (55 metres (60 yds)/100g per skein): 3 skeins red/brown multi #160 (C)
- 12.75mm (size 17) 81.5-cm (32-inch) circular needle or size needed to obtain gauge
- 6.5mm (size K/10½) crochet hook

Gauge
8 sts and 8 rows = 10cm/4 inches in garter st
To save time, take time to check gauge.

Pattern Stitch
Stripe Pattern
Working in garter st, knit
    6 rows B
    4 rows A (3 strands)
    4 rows C
    4 rows B
    4 rows C
    4 rows A (3 strands)
    6 rows B
    Rep these 32 rows for Stripe pat.

Pattern Notes
Circular needle is used to accommodate large number of sts.
    Do not join; work in rows. When working with A, hold 3 strands tog.

Throw
With 3 strands of A held tog, cast on 88 sts.
    Knit 2 rows.
    [Rep 32-row Stripe pat] 5 times.
    Change to A and knit 2 rows.
    Bind off loosely.

Edging
With crochet hook, and 3 strands of A held tog, work 1 row of sc along 1 side edge; do not turn.
    Working from left to right in rev sc, work 1 sc in each sc of previous row.
    Fasten off.
    Rep along opposite side edge. ◆

Counterpane Log Afghan

You'll enjoy stitching this portable project that comes alive when assembled. Knit the triangles individually, sew them into squares and combine the squares.

DESIGN BY FATEMA HABIBUR-RAHMAN

EASY

Finished Size
Approximately 101.5 x 122cm (40 x 48 inches)

Materials
- Plymouth Encore worsted weight 75 per cent acrylic/25 per cent wool yarn (183 metres (200 yds)/100g per ball): 5 balls each beige heather #1415, dark rose #180
- 6mm (size 10) needles or size needed to obtain gauge
- Tapestry needle

4 MEDIUM

Gauge
18 sts and 20 rows = 10cm/4 inches
To save time, take time to check gauge

Special Abbreviations
MB (Make Bobble): In next st [k1, yo, k1, yo, k1, yo, k1], pass 2nd, 3rd, 4th, 5th, 6th, and 7th sts, 1 at a time, over first st.
M1 (Make 1): Inc by knitting in top of st in row below st on needle.

Counterpane Triangles Pattern
Make 60 triangles in each colour (120 triangles)
Cast on 3 sts
Row 1 (RS): K3.
Row 2: P3.
Row 3: M1, k3, M1. (5 sts)
Row 4: Purl.
Row 5: M1, k5, M1. (7 sts)
Row 6: Purl.
Row 7: M1, k3, MB, k3, M1. (9 sts)
Row 8: Purl.
Row 9: M1, k3, MB, k1, MB, k3, M1. (11 sts)
Row 10: Purl.
Row 11: M1, k5, MB, k5, M1. (13 sts)
Row 12: Purl.
Row 13: M1, p13, M1. (15 sts)
Row 14: Knit.
Row 15: M1, p15, M1. (17 sts)
Row 16: Purl.
Row 17: M1, k17, M1. (19 sts)
Row 18: Purl.
Row 19: M1, p19, M1. (21 sts)
Row 20: Knit.
Row 21: M1, p21, M1. (23 sts)
Row 22: Purl.
Row 23: M1, k5, MB, k3, MB, k3, MB, k3, MB, k5, M1. (25 sts)
Row 24: Purl.
Row 25: M1, p25, M1. (27 sts)
Row 26: Knit.
Row 27: M1, p27, M1. (29 sts)
Row 28: Purl.
   Bind off all sts.

Finishing
Referring to photo, sew 4 triangles (2 of each colour) into a square, alternating colours. (30 squares)
   Block squares severely. Each square should measure approximately 20.5 x 20.5cm (8 x 8 inches).
   Sew squares tog, 5 squares wide by 6 squares high. ◆

Maple Leaf Throw

Worked in intarsia, four maple leaves interlock to form a central motif on a quilt-inspired throw. Duplicate stitch outlines each leaf; garter stitch forms the borders.

DESIGN BY DIANE ZANGL

INTERMEDIATE

Finished Size
Approximately 122 x 112cm (48 x 44 inches)

Materials
- Plymouth Encore Worsted Colorspun 75 per cent acrylic/25 per cent wool worsted weight yarn (183 metres (200 yds)/100g per ball): 2 balls rust #7172 (A)
- Plymouth Encore Worsted 75 per cent acrylic/25 per cent wool worsted weight yarn (183 metres (200 yds)/100g per ball): 5 balls dark poplar heather #670 (MC), 1 ball each medium poplar heather #678 (B), autumn red heather #560 (C), gold #1014 (D) and mushroom #240 (E)
- 4.5mm (size 7) 76-cm (30-inch) circular needle or size needed to obtain gauge
- Stitch markers

Gauge
18 sts and 24 rows = 10cm/4 inches in colour pat

To save time, take time to check gauge.

Pattern Notes
Wind separate balls of yarn for each colour area.

To avoid holes when changing colours, always bring new colour up over old.

Throw is worked as 2 panels, each 2 blocks wide by 5 blocks high.

Dark green outline around each leaf is worked in duplicate st after throw is completed.

Throw
Right Panel
With MC, cast on 103 sts.

Sl first st of every RS row, knit 15 rows.

Set up pat:
Next row (RS): Sl 1p wyif, k9 MC, pm, work 41 sts of chart, pm, k7 MC, pm, work 41 sts of chart, pm, k4 MC.

[Sl first st of every RS row and keeping sts between blocks in garter st with MC, work even until 44 rows of chart have been completed. Knit 12 rows with MC only] 4 times.

Work 1 more section of blocks.

With MC, knit 16 rows.

Bind off.

Left Panel
With MC, cast on 103 sts.

Sl first st of every WS row purlwise wyif, knit 15 rows.

Set up pat:
Next row (RS): K4 MC, pm, work 41 sts of chart, pm, k7 MC, pm, work 41 sts of chart, pm, k10 MC.

Sl first st of every WS row, work as for right panel.

Assembly
Referring to chart, work outline around leaves in duplicate st with MC.

Sew panels tog along long unslipped edges. ◆

COLOUR KEY

- ■ Dark poplar heather (MC)
- ■ Rust (A)
- ■ Medium poplar heather (B)
- ■ Autumn red heather (C)
- ■ Gold (D)
- □ Mushroom (E)

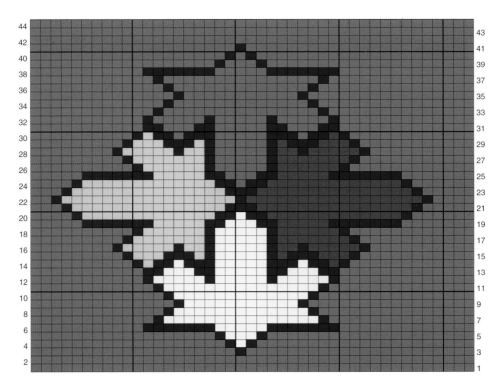

MAPLE LEAF CHART

Monster Mania Pillows

Let these little monsters chase away your end-of-summer blues.

DESIGN BY CELESTE PINHEIRO

EASY

Finished Size
Approximately 90 sq cm (14 inches square)

Materials
- Plymouth Encore Chunky 75 per cent acrylic/25 per cent bulky weight wool yarn (131 metres (143 yds)/100g per ball): 2 balls turquoise #235 (A), 2 balls red #1386 (B), 2 balls royal blue #133 (C), 1 ball each lime green #3335 (D), yellow #1382 (E), white #208 (F)
- 6mm (size 10) straight and double-pointed needles or size needed to obtain gauge
- Stitch holders
- Waste yarn or fibrefill for stuffing
- 4 (2-cm/¾-inch) black buttons
- 5mm (size H/8) crochet hook (for fringe)
- 2 (90-sq-cm/14-inch-square) pillow forms

5 BULKY

Gauge
14 sts = 10cm/4 inches in St st
To save time, take time to check gauge.

Pattern Notes
Yarn amounts given for colours

D, E and F are sufficient for both pillows.

Refer to photo for placement of features.

Hairy

Special Abbreviation
MB (Make Bobble): [K1, p1, k1, p1] into st, pass first 3 sts over last st.

Pattern Stitch
Bobble Knot (multiple of 6 sts +3)
Row 1 (RS): Knit across.
Rows 2, 4, 6, 8 and 10: Purl across.
Row 3: K1, MB, *k5, MB; rep from * to last st, end k1.
Rows 5, 7 and 11: Knit across.
Row 9: K4, MB, *k5, MB; rep from * to last 4 sts, end k4.
Row 12: Purl across.
Rep Rows 1–12 for pat.

Pillow Front
With A, cast on 45 sts. Work in Bobble Knot pat until front measures 35.5cm (14 inches) from beg. Bind off all sts.

Back Flaps
With A, pick up and knit 45 sts along side edge, work in St st

for 18cm (7 inches) from pick-up row, ending with a WS row. Knit 6 rows. Bind off all sts.
Rep for other edge.

Fingers (Toes)
Make 6 of each
Using double-pointed needles and B cast on 3 sts. Slide stitches to the other end of the needle, knit 3 stitches, pulling the yarn across the back of the stitches. Continue to slide the stitches to the other end of the needle and pull the yarn across the back and knit the stitches. Repeat this process until there are 9 rows for the fingers and 12 rows for the toes.

Arm (Leg)
Make 2 of each
With B, knit across sts of 3 shorter (longer) I-cords. (9 sts)
Work even in St st in rows for 18 (23)cm or 7 (9) inches from join. Bind off all sts.
Sew side seam. Sew to pillow.

Eye
Make 2
With F, cast on 5 sts. Working in

St st, inc 1 st at each side [every other row] twice. (9 sts)

Work 2 rows St st. On RS, change to D, knit 2 rows, then work in St st for 6 rows. Dec 1 st at each side [every other row] twice. (5 sts)

Bind off all sts. Sew black button to eye, sew to pillow.

Tooth
Make 3

With F, cast on 9 sts. Working in St st, dec 1 st at each side [every other row] 3 times, then sl 1, k2tog, psso, fasten off.

Embroider mouth with double strand of C and chain st. Sew teeth to pillow.

Fringe

Following fringe instructions on page 8, make single knot fringe. Cut 30.5-cm (12-inch) strands of B, C and D for fringe. Use 1 strand of each for each knot. Referring to photo, tie knots approximately every 5th st around pillow above arms.

Assembly

Sew flaps to front along top and bottom edges, overlapping by 2.5cm (1 inch) at centre. Sew back opening closed, or attach 2 buttons and 2 loops.

Insert pillow form into cover.

Squiggy

Pillow Front

With D, cast on 49 sts.

Triangle pat
Row 1 (RS): Attach C, k1 C, *k7 D, k1 C; rep from * across.

Row 2: P2 C, *p5 D, p3 C; rep from * to last 7 sts, end p5 D, p2 C.
Row 3: K3 C, *k3 D, k5 C; rep from * to last 6 sts, end k3 D, k3 C.
Row 4: P4 C, *p1 D, p7 D; rep from * to last 5 sts, end p1 D, p4 C. Cut D and work in C and St st until front measures 30.5cm (12 inches) from beg, ending with a WS row, inc 1 st on last row. (50 sts)

Cut C, attach E and B.

Beg Stripe Pat
Row 1 (RS): K3 E, k4 B, [k4 E, k4 B] 5 times, k3 E.
Row 2: P3 E, p4 B, [p4 E, p4 B] 5 times, p3 E.
Rep Rows 1 and 2 for pat until front measures 35.5cm (14 inches) from beg. Bind off all sts.

Back Flaps

With C, pick up and knit 49 sts along side edge, work in St st for 18cm (7 inches) from pick-up row, ending with a WS row. Knit 6 rows. Bind off all sts.

Rep for other edge.

Hand (Foot)
Make 8 alike

With D, cast on 4 sts.
Row 1 (WS): Purl across.
Row 2: K1, M1, k2, M1, k1.
Rows 3–5: Work in St st.
Rows 6 and 7: Maintaining St st, cast on 4 sts at beg of row. (14 sts)
Row 8: K1, M1, k12, M1, k1. (16 sts)
Rows 9 and 10: Work in St st.
Row 11: K2tog, k12, ssk. (14 sts)
Purl across, binding off first and last 4 sts. Place rem 6 sts on holder.

Arm (Leg)
Make 2 of each

With RS facing, sl sts of 2 hand (foot) pieces back on needle. With B, knit across 12 sts, then maintaining St st, work 3 more rows B, [4 rows E, 4 rows B] 2 (3) times, end with 4 rows E. Bind off all sts.

Sew hand (foot) halves tog, sew side seam. Stuff with waste E yarn or fibrefill. Sew to pillow.

Eye
Make 2

With F, cast on 6 sts. Working in St st, inc 1 st at each side [every other row] twice. (10 sts)

Work 5 rows St st, ending with a WS row. Dec 1 st at each side [every other row] twice. (6 sts)

Bind off all sts.

Sew button to eye. Sew eye to pillow, stuff with waste F yarn or fibrefill to make it bulge.

Nose

With B, cast on 13 sts. Work in St st, dec 1 st at each side [every other row] 5 times. (3 sts)
Next row: K3tog, fasten off.
Sew nose to pillow.

Mouth

With E, cast on 20 sts.
Row 1 (WS): Purl across.
Row 2: K1, M1, k18, M1, k1. (22 sts)
Rows 3–5: Work in St st.
Row 6: Dec 1 st at each end. (20 sts)
Row 7: Purl across.
Bind off all sts.

Sew mouth to pillow, making it curve a little. With double

CONTINUED ON PAGE 153

Hairy

Squiggy

Nap Time Cosy

Here's an easy-to-knit snuggly blanket created just for your favourite pet!

DESIGN BY CAROL MAY

BEGINNER

Sizes
Small (medium, large, extra-large) instructions are given for smallest size, with larger sizes in parentheses. When only 1 number is given, it applies to all sizes.

Finished Measurements
Width: 30.5 (40.5, 51, 62)cm or 12 (16, 20, 24½) inches
Length: 25.5 (43, 61, 76)cm or 10 (17, 24, 30) inches

Materials
- Plymouth Rimini Rainbow 60 per cent acrylic/40 per cent wool super bulky weight yarn (35 metres (38 yds)/50g per ball): 1 (3, 4, 7) balls #31 (A); 1 (2, 3, 5) balls #27 (B)
- 10mm (size 15) 61-cm (24-inch) circular needle or size needed to obtain gauge
- Additional 10mm (size 15) needle for 3-needle bind off (optional)

- Stitch marker
- Tapestry needle

Gauge
8 sts and 12 rnds = 10cm/4 inches in St st
To save time, take time to check gauge.

Stripe Pattern
Rnd 1: With B, knit.
Rnd 2: With A, knit.
Rep Rnds 1 and 2 for pat.

Blanket
With A, loosely cast on 48 (64, 80, 98) sts.

Join, being careful not to twist stitches, and pm to indicate beg of rnd.

With A, knit 2 rnds.

Work in Stripe pat until piece measures 18 (30.5, 46, 61)cm or 7 (12, 18, 24) inches from beg. Cut B.

Continue working with A *only* until piece measures 25.5 (43, 61, 76)cm or 10 (17, 24, 30) inches, or desired length, from beg.

Bind off using method 1 or 2:
1. Loosely bind off all sts, then turn the tube inside out (purl side will be outside) and sew bottom seam.
2. Work 3-needle bind off as follows: holding the circular needle so that both ends are parallel and pointing to the right, use a spare needle to knit 1 st from each point together; *knit the next 2 sts tog (one from each needle), then pull the first st over the 2nd (1 st bound off); rep from * until all sts are bound off.

Turn the bag inside out so that the purl side is on the outside. ◆

Blue Bands Floor Pillow

This fabric looks great on both sides—choose whichever one you want to be on the outside.

DESIGN BY LOIS S YOUNG

EASY

Finished Size
Approximately 61 x 61cm (24 x 24 inches)

Materials
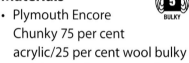

- Plymouth Encore Chunky 75 per cent acrylic/25 per cent wool bulky weight yarn (131 metres (143 yds)/100g per ball): 4 balls blue #598 (A)
- Plymouth Encore Colorspun Chunky 75 per cent acrylic/ 25 per cent wool bulky weight yarn (131 metres (143 yds)/100g per ball): 4 balls blue and peach variegated #7123 (B)
- 6mm (size 10) 73.5-cm (29-inch) circular needle or size needed to obtain gauge
- 155-sq-cm (24-inch-square) pillow form

Gauge
14 sts and 26 rows = 10cm/4 inches in pat
To save time, take time to check gauge.

Pattern Stitch
Row 1 (RS): With B, sl 1, purl to end of row.

Row 2: Sl 1, purl to end of row.
Row 3: Sl 1, knit to end of row. Do not turn, slide sts to other end.
Row 4 (RS): With A, sl 1, purl to end of row.
Row 5: Sl 1, *yo, k2tog; rep from * across. Do not turn, slide sts to other end.
Row 6 (WS): With B, sl 1, knit to end of row.
Row 7: Sl 1, knit to end of row.
Row 8: Sl 1, purl to end of row.
Rows 9–16: Work as for Rows 1–8, exchanging A for B and B for A.
Rep Rows 1–16 for pat.

Pattern Notes
The pattern is made up of 2 8-row sequences with colours reversed.

Each eight-row sequence is worked with 3 rows of one colour, 2 rows of the 2nd colour, then 3 rows of the first colour. This means that at the end of designated rows, you will not turn the work in the normal fashion; rather, you will slide the stitches back to the other end of the needle and begin the next row with the other colour.

Carry yarn not in use up the side.

Pillow
Make 2
With B, cast on 87 sts.
Rows 1 and 2: Sl 1, purl to end of row.
Begin Pattern and work [Rows 1–16] 10 times.
Work Rows 1–8.
Last 2 rows: With B, sl 1, purl to end of row.
Bind off purlwise on RS.

Side Borders
With RS facing and B, pick up and knit 4 sts for each eight-row sequence.
Rows 1 (WS) and 2: Sl 1, knit to end of row.
Bind off knitwise on WS.

Assembly
With RS tog, sew pillow pieces together on 3 sides by overcasting through edge sts.
Turn inside out (if desired) and insert pillow form.
Sew rem side. ✦

Blue Bands Rug

This reversible rug and pillow set is just the thing for leisure-time comfort.

DESIGN BY LOIS S YOUNG

EASY

Finished Size
Approximately 79 x 124.5cm or 31 x 49 inches (excluding fringe)

Materials

- Plymouth Encore Chunky 75 per cent acrylic/25 per cent wool chunky weight yarn (131 metres (143 yds)/100g per ball): 4 balls blue #598 (A)
- Plymouth Encore Colorspun Chunky 75 per cent acrylic/25 per cent wool bulky weight yarn (131 metres (143 yds)/100g per ball): 4 balls blue and peach variegated #7123 (B)
- 6mm (size 10) 73.5-cm (29-inch) circular needle or size needed to obtain gauge
- 3.75mm (size F/5) crochet hook

Gauge
14 sts and 26 rows = 10cm/4 inches in pat
To save time, take time to check gauge.

Pattern Stitch
Row 1 (RS): With B, sl 1, purl to end of row.
Row 2: Sl 1, purl to end of row.
Row 3: Sl 1, knit to end of row. Do not turn, slide sts to other end.
Row 4 (RS): With A, sl 1, purl to end of row.
Row 5: Sl 1, *yo, k2tog; rep from * across. Do not turn, slide sts to other end.
Row 6 (WS): With B, sl 1, knit to end of row.
Row 7: Sl 1, knit to end of row.
Row 8: Sl 1, purl to end of row.
Rows 9–16: Work as for Rows 1–8, exchanging A for B and B for A.
Rep Rows 1–16 for pat.

Pattern Notes
The pattern is made up of 2 8-row sequences with colours reversed.

Each 8-row sequence is worked with 3 rows of one colour, 2 rows of the 2nd colour, then 3 rows of the first colour. This means that at the end of designated rows, you will not turn the work in the normal fashion; rather, you will slide the stitches back to the other end of the needle and begin the next row with the other colour.

Carry yarn not in use up the side.

Rug
With A, cast on 111 sts.
Rows 1 and 2: Sl 1, knit to end of row.
Begin pat st and work [Rows 1–16] 21 times.
Work Rows 1–8.
Last 2 rows: With A, sl 1, purl to end of row.
Bind off purlwise on RS.

Fringe
Following instructions on page 8, attach fringe as follows: Cut 222 23-cm (9-inch) strands of A. Using crochet hook, attach 2-strands-per-fringe in every other st across end of rug. Trim fringe evenly. ✦

Outback Rug

Step onto this soft wool rug and your feet will say, 'Thank you'.

DESIGN BY JOANNE TURCOTTE

EASY

Finished Size
Approximately 91.5cm (36 inches) in diameter

Materials
- Plymouth Outback Wool 100 per cent virgin wool worsted weight yarn (338 metres (370 yds)/200g per skein): 4 skeins grape #959
- 6mm (size 10) double-pointed, 40.5-, 61- and 81.5-cm (16-, 24- and 32-inch) circular needles or size needed to obtain gauge
- 4mm (size G/6) crochet hook

4 MEDIUM

Gauge
16 sts and 32 rnds = 10cm/4 inches in garter st
To save time, take time to check gauge.

Rug
With dpn, cast on 6 sts. Divide evenly onto 3 needles. Join without twisting, pm between first and last st.

Rnd 1: Knit into front and back of each st. (12 sts)

Rnd 2 and all even-numbered rounds: Purl.

Rnd 3: *K1, knit into front and back of next st, pm; rep from * around. (18 sts)

Rnd 5: *K2, knit into front and back of next st; rep from * around. (24 sts)

Rnd 7: *K3, knit into front and back of next st; rep from * around. (30 sts)

Continue to inc every other rnd as established until there are 60 sts between markers, changing to longer needles as necessary and ending with Rnd 2.

Edging
With crochet hook, *ch 6, insert hook into next 3 sts on LH needle and sc them tog; rep from * around. Join with sl st.

Block to soft hexagon shape, flattening edging slightly. ◆

High Times Tea Set

This cheerful tea cosy will add a touch of whimsy to your table while keeping your tea hot longer.

DESIGN BY CHRISTINE L WALTER

EASY

Tea Cosy

Size
Fits a large (8-cups) teapot

Finished Measurement
20.5cm tall x 25.5cm wide (8 inches tall x 10 inches wide)

Materials
- Plymouth Fantasy Naturale 100 per cent mercerised cotton medium weight yarn (128 metres (140 yds)/100g per skein): 1 skein each turquoise #8017 (A), bright variegated #9951 (B), lavender #6399 (C) and tea green #8011 (D)
- 5mm (size 8) needles or size needed to obtain gauge
- Stitch holders
- Tapestry needle

Gauge
18 sts and 24 rows = 10cm/4 inches in Purl-Twist pat
To save time, take time to check gauge.

Special Abbreviation
MB (Make Bobble): Knit into front and back of stitch twice, then knit into front one more time (5 stitches), turn; k5, turn; p5, turn; k5, turn; slip 2nd, 3rd, 4th and 5th sts over the first st, k1.

Pattern Stitches
A. Bobble Edging (multiple of 6 sts + 5 sts)
Row 1 (RS): K2, * MB, k5; rep from *, end MB, k2.
Rows 2–4: Knit.
B. Purl-Twist Pattern (multiple of 2 sts)
Rows 1 and 3 (RS): Knit.
Row 2: *P2tog, but do not slip from needle; purl first st again, then slip both sts from needle tog; rep from * across.
Row 4: P1; rep from * on Row 2 across to last st, end p1.
Rep Rows 1–4 for pat.

Side
Make 2
With A, cast on 47 sts.
Work 4 rows of Bobble Edging, dec 1 st on last row. Cut A. (46 sts)
With B, work Purl-Twist pat, working [4 row rep] 7 times, then work first 2 rows once more. Cut B.

Shape Top
Row 1 (RS): With A, knit.
Row 2: Knit.
Row 3: K2, *k2tog, k2; rep from * across. (35 sts)
Rows 4–8: Knit.
Row 9: K1, *K2tog, k1; rep from * to last st, end k1. (24 sts)
Rows 10–14: Knit.
Row 15: K2tog across. (12 sts)
Rows 16–18: Knit.
Row 19: K2tog across. (6 sts)
Cut A, leaving a long tail. Put sts on holder.

Large Rose
With C and leaving a long tail, cast on 80 sts.
Beg with a RS row, work in St st for 2.5cm (1 inch).
Dec over next three rows as follows:
Row 1: K2tog across. (40 sts)
Row 2: P2tog across. (20 sts)
Row 3: K2tog across. (10 sts)
Cut yarn, leaving a long tail. Using a tapestry needle, thread tail through rem sts and pull up into gathers. Form rose by twisting the piece round and round from the centre, with RS facing out. Pull the rose into shape as you go, letting

the fabric roll over. Sew layers together by working a few stitches through all the layers at the bottom to hold them in place.

Small Rose

With C and leaving a long tail, cast on 60 sts.

Beg with a RS row, work in St st for 2.5cm (1 inch).

Dec over next three rows as follows:

Row 1: K2tog across. (30 sts)
Row 2: P2tog across. (15 sts)
Row 3: K2tog across to last st, end k1. (8 sts)

Cut yarn, leaving a long tail. Continue as for large rose.

Leaves
Make 3

With D and leaving long tails, cast on 3 sts.
Row 1 (WS): Purl.
Row 2 (RS): K1, yo, k1, yo, k1. (5 sts)
Row 3 and all WS rows: Purl.
Row 4: K2, yo, k1, yo, k2. (7 sts)
Row 6: K3, yo, k1, yo, k3. (9 sts)
Row 8: K4, yo, k1, yo, k4. (11 sts)
Row 10: Ssk, k7, k2tog. (9 sts)
Row 12: Ssk, k5, k2tog. (7 sts)
Row 14: Ssk, k3, k2tog. (5 sts)

Row 16: Ssk, k1, k2tog. (3 sts)
Row 18: Sk2p.

Cut yarn and pull through the last st.

Weave in tail at top of leaf, reserving yarn tail at stem end for sewing leaf to cosy.

Assembly

Using a tapestry needle, weave tail at top of the first piece through the live stitches of the 2nd piece and vice versa. Pull tight to close top.

Sew garter portion of cosy at each side of centre top.

Place cosy on teapot and mark openings for spout and handle before sewing up sides. Using mattress st, sew sides, leaving sections between markers open.

Sew roses and leaves to centre top of tea cosy.

Hot Pads

Finished Measurement
48 sq cm (7½ inches square)

Materials
- Plymouth Fantasy Naturale 100 per cent mercerised cotton medium

4
MEDIUM

weight yarn (100g/140 yds per skein): 1 ball each of #6399 lavender (C) and #8011 tea green (D)
- 5mm (size 8) needles or size needed to obtain gauge
- 5mm (size H/8) crochet hook
- Tapestry needle

Side One
Make 2

With C, cast on 34 sts.
Knit 4 rows.
Change to Purl-Twist pat and work [4 row rep] 10 times.
Knit 3 rows.
Bind off knitwise on WS.

Side Two
Make 2

Work as for Side One, but bind off until 1 st rem.

Loop

Using crochet hook, chain-10 in last st. Work slip st into first st, then fasten off.

Assembly

With RS facing out, sew the two sides tog. ◆

Face Cloth Quartet

Each face cloth only uses one ball of yarn.

DESIGN BY FRANCES HUGHES

Leafy Green Ladders Cloth

EASY

Finished Size
Approximately 55 sq cm
(8½ inches square)

Materials

MEDIUM
- JCA/Reynolds Saucy 100 per cent cotton worsted weight yarn (169 metres (185 yds)/100g per ball): 1 ball lt. emerald #11
- 5mm (size 8) needles or size needed to obtain gauge
- Tapestry needle

Gauge
9 sts and 10 rows = 5cm/2 inches in pat
To save time, take time to check gauge.

Pattern Note
Slip all sts purlwise with yarn on WS of fabric.

Instructions
Cast on 41 sts.

Border
Row 1: *K2tog, yo; rep from * to last st, end k1.
Rows 2–4: K1, *yo, k2tog; rep from * across.

Body
Foundation row: [K2tog, yo] twice, k1, purl across to last 5 sts, end k1, [yo, k2tog] twice.
Row 1 (RS): K1, [yo, k2tog] twice, k3, *sl 1, k3; rep from * to last 5 sts, end k1, [yo, k2tog] twice.
Row 2: K1, [yo, k2tog] twice, *k3, sl 1, k3; rep from * across to last 5 sts, end k1, [yo, k2tog] twice.
Row 3: K1, [yo, k2tog] twice, k1, sl 1, *k3, sl 1; rep from * to last 6 sts, end k2, [yo, k2tog] twice.
Row 4: K1, [yo, k2tog] twice, p1, sl 1, *p3, sl 1; rep from * across to last 6 sts, end p1, k1, [yo, k2tog] twice.
Work [Rows 1–4] 7 times, then rep Rows 1–4 of border. Bind off all sts.

Cherry Red Boxes Cloth

BEGINNER

Finished Size
Approximately 58 sq cm
(9 inches square)

Materials

MEDIUM
- JCA/Reynolds Saucy 100 per cent cotton worsted weight yarn (100g/185 yds per ball): 1 ball crimson #361
- 5mm (size 8) needles or size needed to obtain gauge
- Tapestry needle

Gauge
9 sts and 12 rows = 5cm/2 inches in pat
To save time, take time to check gauge.

Instructions
Cast on 41 sts.

Border
Knit 4 rows.

Body
Row 1 (RS): K4, p3, *k3, p3; rep from * to last 4 sts, end k4.
Row 2: K3, p1, k3, *p3, k3; rep from * to last 4 sts, end p1, k3.
Row 3: K4, yo, k3tog, yo, *k3, yo, k3tog, yo; rep from * to last 4 sts, end k4.

Row 4: K3, purl across to last 3 sts, end k3.

Row 5: K7, p3, *k3, p3; rep from * to last 7 sts, end k7.

Row 6: K3, p4, k3, *p3, k3; rep from * to last 7 sts, end p4, k3.

Row 7: K7, yo, k3tog, yo, *k3, yo, k3tog, yo; rep from * to last 7 sts, end k7.

Row 8: Rep Row 4.

Work [Rows 1–8] 6 times.

Knit 4 rows. Bind off all sts.

Golden Acorns Cloth

Finished Size

Approximately 21.5cm (8½ inches)

Materials

- JCA/Reynolds Saucy 100 per cent cotton worsted weight yarn (169 metres (185 yds)/100g per ball): 1 ball sunburst #130
- 5mm (size 8) needles
- Tapestry needle

Gauge

9 sts and 12 rows = 5cm/2 inches in seed st

To save time, take time to check gauge.

Special Abbreviation

M3 (Make 3): [K1, p1, k1] in next st.

Instructions

Cast on 41 sts.

Border

Rows 1–5: *K1, p1; rep from * across.

Body

Row 1 (RS): [K1, p1] twice, p3, *k3, p3; rep from * to last 4 sts, end [p1, k1] twice.

Row 2: [K1, p1] twice, k3, *p3, k3; rep from * to last 4 sts, end [p1, k1] twice.

Row 3: [K1, p1] twice, p1, M3, p1, *sl 1, k2tog, psso, p1, M3, p1; rep from * to last 4 sts, end [p1, k1] twice.

Row 4: [K1, p1] twice, k1, p3, *k3, p3; rep from * to last 5 sts, end k1, [p1, k1] twice.

Row 5: [K1, p1] twice, p1, k3, *p3, k3; rep from * to last 5 sts, end p1, [p1, k1] twice.

Row 6: Rep Row 4.

Row 7: [K1, p1] twice, p1, sl 1, k2tog, psso, p1, *M3, p1, sl 1, k2tog, psso, p1; rep from * to last 4 sts, [p1, k1] twice.

Row 8: Rep Row 2.

Work [Rows 1–8] 5 times.

Rep border Rows 1–5. Bind off all sts.

Diamonds Raspberry Cloth

Finished Size

Approximately 58 sq cm (9 inches square)

Materials

- JCA/Reynolds Saucy 100 per cent cotton worsted weight yarn (169 metres (185 yds)/100g per ball): 1 ball boysen berry #624
- 5mm (size 8) needles
- Tapestry needle

Gauge

8 sts and 6 rows = 5cm/2 inches in pat

To save time, take time to check gauge.

Instructions

Cast on 43 sts.

Border

Rows 1–3: *K1, p1; rep from * across.

Body

Row 1 (RS): K1, p1, k1, *[k3, p1] twice, k1, p1; rep from * to last 10 sts, end k3, p1, k4, p1, k1.

Row 2: K1, p1, k1, *[p3, k1] twice, p1, k1; rep from * to last 10 sts, p3, k1, p3, k1, p1, k1.

Row 3: K1, p1, k3, p1, k1, p1, *[k3, p1] twice, k1, p1; rep from * to last 5 sts, end k3, p1, k1.

Row 4: K1, p1, k1, p2, k1, p1, k1, *[p3, k1] twice, p1, k1; rep from * to last 5 sts, end p2, k1, p1, k1.

Row 5: K1, p1, k1, [k1, p1] 3 times, *[k2, p1] twice; [k1, p1] twice; rep from * to last 4 sts, end k2, p1, k1.

Row 6: K1, p1, k1, [p1, k1] 3 times, *[p2, k1] twice; [p1, k1] twice; rep from * to last 4 sts, [p1, k1] twice.

Row 7: Rep Row 3.
Row 8: Rep Row 4.
Row 9: Rep Row 1.
Row 10: Rep Row 2.
Row 11: K1, p1, k4, p1, *k2, [p1, k1] twice, p1, k2, p1; rep from * to last 6 sts, end k4, p1, k1.
Row 12: K1, p1, k1, p3, k1, *p2, [k1, p1] twice, k1, p2, k1; rep from * to last 6 sts, end p3, k1, p1, k1.
Work [Rows 1–12] 4 times.

Border
Rep border Rows 1–3. Bind off all sts. ✦

Little Fringes

Nifty fringes are created as-you-go. When you're done, you're DONE!

DESIGN BY KENNITA TULLY

EASY

Finished Sizes
Place Mat: approximately 42 x 30.5cm or 16½ x 12 inches (excluding fringe)
Glass Cosy: approximately 10cm high and 17cm around or 4 inches x 6¾ inches (excluding fringe)

Materials
- Plymouth Bella Colour 55 per cent cotton/45 per cent acrylic medium weight yarn (95 metres (104 yds)/50g per ball): 2 balls blue #17 per set (place mat and glass cosy)
- 6mm (size 10) needles or size needed to obtain gauge
- Tapestry needle

Gauge
16 sts and 28 rows = 10cm/4 inches in St st
To save time, take time to check gauge.

Pattern Notes
Long tail and cable cast-on are used in this pattern.

The fringes are created by casting on, then immediately binding off 8 sts at each end as indicated.

Place Mat
Using long tail method, cast on 84 sts.
Row 1 (WS): Bind off 8 sts, knit across row. (76 sts)
Row 2: Bind off 8 sts, knit across row. (68 sts)
Rows 3 and 5: Purl.
Row 4: Knit.
Row 6: Knit across row; turn and cable cast on 8 sts. (76 sts)
Row 7: Bind off 8 sts, knit across row; turn and cable cast on 8 sts. (76 sts)
Row 8: Bind off 8 sts, knit across row. (68 sts)

Rows 9 and 11: Purl.
Row 10: Knit.
Rep [Rows 6–11] 10 more times.
    Work Rows 6 and 7.
    Bind off.

Glass Cosy
Using long tail method, cast on 24 sts.
Row 1: Bind off 8 sts, knit across row. (16 sts)
Rows 2 and 4: Knit.
Rows 3 and 5: Purl.
Row 6: Knit across row, turn and cable cast on 8 sts. (24 sts)
Row 7: Bind off 8 sts, knit across row. (16 sts)
Rep [Rows 2–7] 5 more times.
    Work Rows 2–5.
    Bind off.
    Sew cast-on and bind-off edges together. ◆

Bowknot Table Set

Enjoy a new stitch pattern while making this charming table set.

DESIGN BY SCARLET TAYLOR

BEGINNER

Finished Size
Place Mat: 51 x 31.5cm (20½ x 12½ inches)
Coaster: 32 sq cm (5 inches square)
Napkin Ring: 16.5 x 7.5cm (6½ x 3 inches wide)

Materials
- Brown Sheep Cotton Fleece 80 per cent Prima cotton/20 per cent merino wool light worsted weight yarn (197 metres (215 yds)/100g per skein): 2 skeins antique lace #CW-150
- 4mm (size 6) straight needles, 2 double-pointed needles (for edging) or size needed to obtain gauge
- Tapestry needle

Gauge
20 sts and 28 rows = 10cm/4 inches in pat
To save time, take time to check gauge.

Special Abbreviation
Make 1 (M1): Inc by making a backward loop on the RH ndl.

Pattern Stitches
A. Tiny Bowknot Stitch (place mat and coaster)

Rows 1 and 5 (WS): Sl 1, purl to end.
Rows 2 and 6: Sl 1, knit to end.
Row 3: Sl 1, p2, *k3, p3; rep from * across.
Row 4: Sl 1, k2, *p1, k1 into st in row below, dropping loop on ndl, p1, k3; rep from * across.
Row 7: Sl 1, p5, *k3, p3; rep from *, end p3.
Row 8: Sl 1, k5, *p1, k1 into st in row below, dropping loop on ndl, p1, k3; rep from *, end k3.
Rep Rows 1–8 for pat.

B. Tiny Bowknot Stitch (napkin ring)
Rows 1, 2, 5 and 6: Work as above.
Row 3: Sl 1, p1, *k3, p3; rep from *, end p2 instead of p3.
Row 4: Sl 1, k1, *p1, k1 into st in row below, dropping loop on ndl, p1, k3; rep from *, end k2 instead of k3.
Row 7: Sl 1, p4, *k3, p3; rep from *, end p2.
Row 8: Sl 1, k4, *p1, k1 into st in row below, dropping loop on ndl, p1, k3; rep from *, end k2.

C. Edging
Note: When working edging, sl all sts knitwise and turn work at end of each row.

Use 2 dpn. Cast on 3 sts.
Row 1 (WS): K2, sl 1, pick up 1 st from edge of article.
Row 2: K2tog, k1, M1, k1. (4 sts)
Row 3: K3, sl 1, pick up 1 st from edge of article.
Row 4: K2tog, k2, M1, k1. (5 sts)
Row 5: K4, sl 1, pick up 1 st from edge of article.
Row 6: K2tog, k4.
Row 7: K4, sl 1, pick up 1 st from edge of article.
Row 8: K2tog, k1, k2tog, k1. (4 sts)
Row 9: K3, sl 1, pick up 1 st from edge of article.
Row 10: K2tog, k2tog, k1. (3 sts)
Row 11: K2, sl 1, pick up 1 st from edge of article.
Row 12: K2tog, k2.
Rep Rows 1–12 for edging.

Pattern Note
Sl first st of each row purlwise on RS rows and knitwise on WS rows.

Place Mat
Cast on 99 sts. Work [Rows 1–8 of pat A] 10 times. Rep Rows 1–6. Bind off all sts purlwise.

Edging

With WS of mat facing, beg 1 st after corner st on side edge. Work edging along side, picking up 1 attaching st in each edge st. At corner, attach Rows 1–12 of edging all into same st.

Continue working edging along top or bottom, skipping 1 edge st when attaching edging on Rows 1 and 7. Work corner to match first one. Continue edging in this manner around entire mat. After final corner is turned, bind off rem sts. Sew end of edging to beg. Block.

Coaster

Cast on 21 sts. Work [Rows 1–8 of pat A] 3 times. Rep Rows 1–6. Bind off all sts purlwise.

Work edging as for place mat, but attach edging to every edge st across top and bottom edges. Block.

Napkin Ring

Cast on 31 sts. Work Rows 1–8 of pat B, then rep Rows 1–6. Bind off all sts purlwise.

Work edging along top and bottom edges, attaching it in every edge st. Sew sides tog to form circle. Block. ✦

Starburst Table Mat

Add sparkle to your table with this out-of-the-ordinary shaped mat.

DESIGN BY SUE CHILDRESS

EASY

Finished Size

Approximately 40.5cm (16 inches) diameter

Materials

- Plymouth Fantasy Naturale 100 per cent mercerised cotton worsted weight yarn (128 metres (140 yds)/100g per skein): 1 skein blue/green variegated #9936
- 4.5mm (size 7) double-pointed, 40.5- and 61-cm (16- and 24-inch) circular needles or size needed to obtain gauge
- Stitch marker

Gauge

12 sts and 22 rnds = 10cm/4 inches in St st after blocking
To save time, take time to check gauge.

Pattern Note

Change to longer needles when necessary.

Table Mat

With dpn, cast on 8 sts. Divide evenly onto 4 needles. Join without twisting, pm between first and last st.

Rnds 1, 3, 5 and 7: *Yo, k1; rep from * around.

Rnds 2, 4, 6, 8, 10 and 12: Knit.

Rnd 9: *K2, yo; rep from * around. (192 sts)

Rnd 11: *K4, yo; rep from * around. (240 sts)

Rnd 13: *K2tog, k1; rep from * around. (160 sts)

Rnd 14: Purl.

Rnd 15: *P2tog, p3; rep from * around. (128 sts)

Rnd 16: Purl.

Rnd 17: *P2tog, p2; rep from * around. (96 sts)

Rnds 18–21: Knit.

Rnd 22: *K6, yo; rep from * around. (112 sts)

Rnds 23, 25, 27 and 29: Knit.

Rnd 24: *K7, yo; rep from * around. (128 sts)

Rnd 26: *K8, yo; rep from * around. (144 sts)

Rnd 28: *K4, yo, k5, yo; rep from * around. (176 sts)

Rnd 30: *K5, yo, k6, yo; rep from * around. (208 sts)

Rnds 31–32: Knit.
    Bind off purlwise.
    Wet-block, pulling points into place. ◆

Mr Flurry

This fun and friendly snowman would look great decorating your table or your mantel all winter.

DESIGN BY MICHELE WILCOX

EASY

Finished Measurement
Approximately 28cm (11 inches) high, including hat

Materials
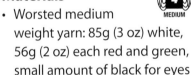
- Worsted medium weight yarn: 85g (3 oz) white, 56g (2 oz) each red and green, small amount of black for eyes
- 5mm (size 8) needles or size needed to obtain gauge
- Stuffing
- Tapestry needle
- Crochet hook (for fringe)

Gauge
17 sts = 10cm/4 inches in St st
To save time, take time to check gauge.

Body
Beg at bottom, with white, cast on 20 sts.
Row 1 (RS): [K1, inc 1] in each st across. (40 sts)
Row 2 and all rem WS rows: Purl.
Row 3: Rep Row 1. (80 sts)
Rows 5–36: Work even in St st.

Row 37: *K2, k2tog; rep from * across. (60 sts)
Row 39: *K1, k2tog; rep from * across. (40 sts)
Rows 41–62: Work even in St st.
Row 63: *K2, k2tog; rep from * across. (30 sts)
Row 65: *K1, k2tog; rep from * across. (20 sts)
Row 66: Purl.
Cut yarn leaving a 38-cm (15-inch) end. Using tapestry needle, thread yarn through rem sts, pull tight, then sew back seam.
Stuff body, gather bottom sts and pull tight; fasten off securely.
Shape body.
With black, embroider eyes.

Hat
With red, cast on 44 sts.
Rows 1–10: Work in k2, p2 ribbing.
Rows 11–32: Beg with a knit row, work even in St st.
Row 33 (RS): *K2, k2tog; rep from * across. (33 sts)
Row 34: Purl.
Row 35: *K1, k2tog; rep from *

across. (22 sts)
Row 36: Purl.
Cut yarn leaving a 25.5-cm (10-inch) end. Using tapestry needle, thread yarn through rem sts, pull tight, then sew back seam.
Make a small green pompom and fasten to top of hat.

Scarf
With green, cast on 13 sts.
Row 1: K1, *p1, k1; rep from * across.
Rep Row 1 for seed st until scarf measures 53.5cm (21 inches) long. Bind off all sts.

Fringe
Wrap yarn 42 times around a 5-cm (2-inch) wide piece of cardboard; cut along 1 edge. *Fold 3 strands in half, pull lp through st with crochet hook, pull ends through lp, pull snug. Rep from * in every other st across both ends of scarf. Trim ends even. ✦

Knitting Angel

This angel is dressed in her knitted best, with her project in progress.

DESIGN BY KATHY PERRY

EASY

Size
Approximately 38cm (15 inches) tall

Materials
- Lion Brand Glitterspun 60 per cent acrylic/27 per cent Cupro/13 per cent polyester worsted weight metallic yarn (105 metres (115 yds)/50g per ball): 1 ball gold #170 (A)
- Lion Brand Fun Fur 100 per cent polyester bulky weight eyelash yarn (55 metres (60 yds)/50g per ball): 1 ball ivory #098 (B)
- Lion Brand Microspun 100 per cent micro-fiber acrylic sport weight yarn (154 metres (168 yds)/70g per ball): 1 ball lily white #100 (C)
- 3.5mm (size 4) needles
- 5mm (size 8) needles or size needed to obtain gauge
- 6.5mm (size 10½) needles
- Egg-shaped foam ball: Approximately 9 x 10cm (3½ x 4 inches)
- 2-litre plastic bottle
- 450-g (16-oz) package dried beans or other weight
- 6.5-cm wide (2½-inch) wire-edged ribbon: 90cm (1 yd) white

- 5-mm wide (¼-inch) rickrack: 45cm (½ yd) gold
- Small wooden beads: 2 dark blue or black
- 2 toothpicks or wire pieces, cut to 5cm (2 inches)
- 5 Snowflake sequins
- Miscellaneous scrap yarn
- Needle and thread
- Scissors
- Fabric or craft glue
- Blush
- Holiday decoration and knitting charms (optional for base)

Gauge
18 sts and 26 rows = 10cm/4 inches in St st with A and 5mm (size 8) needles
16 sts and 20 rows = 10cm/4 inches in St st with B and 6.5mm (size 10½) needles
24 sts and 32 rows = 10cm/4 inches in St st with C and 3.5mm (size 4) needles
To save time, take time to check gauge.

Dress
With 5mm (size 8) needles and A, cast on 68 sts, leaving a long tail of yarn. Work in St st until piece measures 28cm (11 inches).

Bind off.
Seam sides tog to make tube, leaving tail.

Hat
With 5mm (size 8) needles and A, cast on 59 sts, leaving a long tail of yarn. Work in St st until piece measures 7.5cm (3 inches). Change to B and 6.5mm (size 10½) needles and continue for 2.5cm (1 inch). Bind off.
Seam sides tog. Use top tail to gather top edge and secure tightly. Add a small pompom using B.

Cape
With 6.5mm (size 10½) needles and B, cast on 80 sts, leaving a long tail of yarn. Work in St st until piece measures 10cm (4 inches). Bind off, leaving a long tail of yarn. Seam sides tog, making tube. Tails will be used to gather both open ends of cape.

Head
With 3.5cm (size 4) needles and C, cast on 75 sts, leaving a long tail of yarn. Work in St st until piece measures 15cm (6 inches). Bind off, leaving a long tail of yarn. Using 1 tail,

gather end tightly, then seam sides tog, leaving other end open.

Arms

With 3.5mm (size 4) needles and C, cast on 12 sts, leaving a long tail of yarn. Work in St st until piece measures 15cm (6 inches). Bind off, leaving a long tail of yarn. Roll to make arm, sew seam. Gather both ends tightly and secure, leaving a long tail.

Assembly

Cut off top of plastic bottle 2.5cm (1 inch) down from neck. Make 1 hole in each side 2.5cm (1 inch) down from cut edge. Fill bottle with dried beans for weight.

Make head by putting knitted head piece over foam

egg and gathering and securing bottom tightly. Place head into bottle so that bottom sits approximately 2–2.5cm (¾–1 inch) below opening.

Fasten arms in place by using yarn tails to tack arms to both sides of head, going through holes in bottle. Make sure head and arms are secure. Pull dress over bottom of bottle, positioning it so that bottom rolls up naturally. Gather top to fit bottle and secure. Put cape over dress and gather both ends to fit and secure. Tack top of cape to head with needle and thread where ears and mouth would be. Place hat on head and glue in place. Glue rickrack around hat for halo.

Tie ribbon into large bow and place on back of angel for wings. Pin or glue in place. Place hands tog and tack in place.

Make small knitting needles with 2 toothpicks or pieces of

wire. Glue wooden beads on ends. With scrap yarn and small needles, make a knitted piece approximately 2.5 x 4cm (1 x 1½ inches) to place on toothpick needles, leaving a long end to roll into a yarn ball. Place needles in angel's hands and glue to secure.

Add beads for eyes and make cheeks with tiny amount of blush. Glue sequins randomly on angel. Secure yarn ball and add holiday decoration and knitting charms to base if desired. Add glue to any needed areas to secure final assembly. ◆

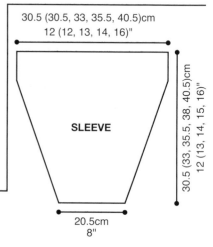

Smiley Face Cardigan
Continued from page 14

Beg at bottom of right front with CC, RS facing, pick up and knit approximately 33 (36, 42) sts to shoulder, knit across 10 (12, 12) sts from back neck holder, pick up and knit approximately 33 (36, 42) sts from shoulder to left front hem. Knit 1 row.

Buttonholes: K2 (2, 3), yo, k2tog, [k5 (6, 7), yo, k2tog] twice, knit to end.

Knit 1 row. Bind off.

Sew buttons to left front to correspond with buttonholes. ◆

Making a Wish
Continued from page 16

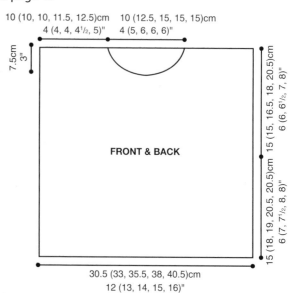

Weekender Jumper
Continued from page 25

Work even for 15cm (6 inches), ending with a WS row.

Dec row: K1, ssk, knit to last 3 sts, k2 tog, k1.

Continue to work in St st, rep dec row [every 8th row] 4 times more. (70, 70, 70, 76, 76 sts)

Work even in St st for 7 rows, ending with a RS row. Knit 3 rows. Bind off all sts.

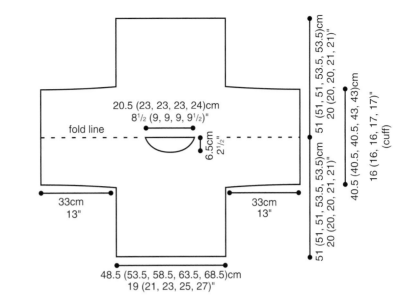

20.5 (23, 23, 23, 24)cm
8½ (9, 9, 9, 9½)"

fold line

6.5cm
2½"

51 (51, 51, 53.5, 53.5)cm
20 (20, 20, 21, 21)"

40.5 (40.5, 40.5, 43, 43)cm
16 (16, 16, 17, 17)" (cuff)

51 (51, 51, 53.5, 53.5)cm
20 (20, 20, 21, 21)"

33cm
13"

33cm
13"

51 (51, 51, 53.5, 53.5)cm
20 (20, 20, 21, 21)"

48.5 (53.5, 58.5, 63.5, 68.5)cm
19 (21, 23, 25, 27)"

Assembly
Sew side and sleeve seams. With circular needle, attach yarn, pick up and knit around neck at a rate of 3 sts for every 4 rows.

Join, purl 1 rnd, knit 1 rnd, purl 1 rnd. Bind off all sts knitwise.

Rep for waistband. ◆

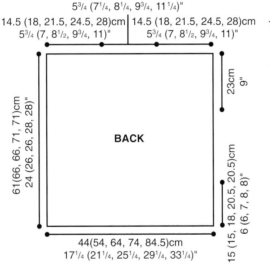

14.5 (18.5, 21, 24.5, 28.5)cm
5¾ (7¼, 8¼, 9¾, 11¼)"

14.5 (18, 21.5, 24.5, 28)cm
5¾ (7, 8½, 9¾, 11)"

14.5 (18, 21.5, 24.5, 28)cm
5¾ (7, 8½, 9¾, 11)"

23cm
9"

BACK

61(66, 66, 71, 71)cm
24 (26, 26, 28, 28)"

15 (15, 18, 20.5, 20.5)cm
6 (6, 7, 8, 8)"

44(54, 64, 74, 84.5)cm
17¼ (21¼, 25¼, 29¼, 33¼)"

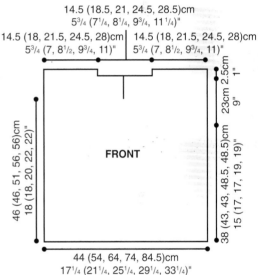

14.5 (18.5, 21, 24.5, 28.5)cm
5¾ (7¼, 8¼, 9¾, 11¼)"

14.5 (18, 21.5, 24.5, 28)cm
5¾ (7, 8½, 9¾, 11)"

14.5 (18, 21.5, 24.5, 28)cm
5¾ (7, 8½, 9¾, 11)"

2.5cm
1"

FRONT

46 (46, 51, 56, 56)cm
18 (18, 20, 22, 22)"

23cm
9"

38 (43, 43, 48.5, 48.5)cm
15 (17, 17, 19, 19)"

44 (54, 64, 74, 84.5)cm
17¼ (21¼, 25¼, 29¼, 33¼)"

Weave a Little Colour
Continued from page 64

Using yarn needle, thread yarn end through all sts and pull tight. Fasten off securely.

Thumb
Sl 4 sts from holder to first needle, pick up and knit 8 sts around thumb opening, placing 4 on each rem needle. Work in K2, P2 Rib until thumb measures 7.5 (9)cm or 3 (3½) inches. Cut yarn.

Using yarn needle, thread yarn end through all sts and pull tight. Fasten off securely. ◆

Monster Mania Pillows
Continued from page 126

strand of B, embroider chain st around mouth.

Assembly
Sew flaps to front along top and bottom edge, overlapping by 2.5cm (1 inch) at centre. Sew back opening closed, or attach 2 buttons and 2 loops.

Insert pillow form into cover. ◆

INDEX

Family Fashions

Cruising the Neighbourhood, 10

Strut Your Stuff, 12

Smiley Face Cardigan, 14

Making a Wish, 16

Weekender Jumper, 25

Team Spirit Jumper, 18

Like Father, Like Son, 21

Checks & Stripes Twin Set, 26

Peachy Party Cardigan, 31

Sheer Stripings Tunic, 34

In My Denims, 37

Hot Chocolate Jumper, 40

In the Holiday Spirit, 43

Blazer Style Cardigan, 46

Easy Zoom Jacket, 49

INDEX

INDEX

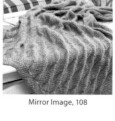

INDEX

Standard Abbreviations

[ ] work instructions within brackets as many times as directed
( ) work instructions within parentheses in the place directed
** repeat instructions following the asterisks as directed
* repeat instructions following the single asterisk as directed
" inch(es)

beg begin/beginning
CC contrasting colour
ch chain stitch
cm centimetre(s)
cn cable needle
dec decrease/decreases/decreasing
dpn(s) double-pointed needle(s)
g gram
inc increase/increases/increasing
k knit
k2tog knit 2 stitches together
LH left hand
lp(s) loop(s)
m metre(s)
M1 make one stitch
MC main colour
mm millimetre(s)
oz ounce(s)
p purl
pat(s) pattern(s)
p2tog purl 2 stitches together
pm place marker
psso pass slipped stitch over
p2sso pass 2 slipped stitches over
rem remain/remaining
rep repeat(s)
rev St st reverse Stockinette stitch
RH right hand
rnd(s) round(s)
RS right side
skp slip, knit, pass stitch over—one stitch decreased
sk2p slip 1, knit 2 together, pass slip stitch over the knit 2 together—2 stitches have been decreased
sl slip
sl 1k slip 1 knitwise
sl 1p slip 1 purlwise
sl st slip stitch(es)
ssk slip, slip, knit these 2 stitches together—a decrease
sq cm square centimetre(s)
st(s) stitch(es)
St st Stockinette stitch/ stocking stitch
tbl through back loop(s)
tog together
WS wrong side
wyib with yarn in back
wyif with yarn in front
yd(s) yard(s)
yfwd yarn forward
yo yarn over

INCHES INTO MILLIMETRES & CENTIMETRES (Rounded off slightly)

mm	cm	inches	cm	inches	cm	inches	cm	inches
3	0.3	1/8	12.5	5	53.5	21	96.5	38
6	0.6	1/4	14	5 1/2	56	22	99	39
10	1	3/8	15	6	58.5	23	101.5	40
13	1.3	1/2	18	7	61	24	104	41
15	1.5	5/8	20.5	8	63.5	25	106.5	42
20	2	3/4	23	9	66	26	109	43
22	2.2	7/8	25.5	10	68.5	27	112	44
25	2.5	1	28	11	71	28	114.5	45
32	3.2	1 1/4	30.5	12	73.5	29	117	46
38	3.8	1 1/2	33	13	76	30	119.5	47
45	4.5	1 3/4	35.5	14	79	31	122	48
50	5	2	38	15	81.5	32	124.5	49
65	6.5	2 1/2	40.5	16	84	33	127	50
75	7.5	3	43	17	86.5	34	129.5	51
90	9	3 1/2	46	18	89	35	132	52
100	10	4	48.5	19	91.5	36	134.5	53
115	11.5	4 1/2	51	20	94	37	137	54

KNITTING NEEDLES CONVERSION CHART

Metric (mm)	2	2.25	2.75	3.25	3.5	3.75	4	4.5	5	5.5	6	6.5	8	9	10
Canada/US	0	1	2	3	4	5	6	7	8	9	10	10½	11	13	15

CROCHET HOOKS CONVERSION CHART

Metric (mm)	2.25	2.75	3.25	3.5	3.75	4.25	5	5.5	6	6.5	9.0
Canada/US	1/B	2/C	3/D	4/E	5/F	6/G	8/H	9/I	10/J	10½/K	N

Skill Levels

BEGINNER	EASY	INTERMEDIATE	EXPERIENCED
Projects for first-time knitters using basic knit and purl stitches. Minimal shaping.	Projects using basic stitches, repetitive stitch patterns, simple colour changes and simple shaping and finishing.	Projects with a variety of stitches, such as basic cables and lace, simple intarsia, double-pointed needles and knitting in the round needle techniques, mid-level shaping and finishing.	Projects using advanced techniques and stitches, such as short rows, Fair Isle, more intricate intarsia, cables, lace patterns and numerous colour changes.

Standard Yarn Weight System

Categories of yarn, gauge ranges and recommended needle sizes

Yarn Weight Symbol & Category Names	1 SUPER FINE	2 FINE	3 LIGHT	4 MEDIUM	5 BULKY	6 SUPER BULKY
Type of Yarns in Category	Sock, Fingering, Baby	Sport, Baby	DK, Light Worsted	Worsted, Afghan, Aran	Chunky, Craft, Rug	Bulky, Roving
Knit Gauge* Ranges in Stockinette Stitch to 10cm (4 inches)	21–32 sts	23–26 sts	21–24 sts	16–20 sts	12–15 sts	6–11 sts
Recommended Needle in Metric Size Range	2.25–3.25mm	3.25–3.75mm	3.75–4.5mm	4.5–5.5mm	5.5–8mm	8mm
Recommended Needle Canada/US Size Range	1 to 3	3 to 5	5 to 7	7 to 9	9 to 11	11 and larger

* GUIDELINES ONLY: The above reflect the most commonly used gauges and needle sizes for specific yarn categories.